OPEN THE DECK

A step-by-step procedure for writing

by

Tanis Knight and Larry Lewin

The Stack the Deck Writing Program
Tinley Park, Illinois

Acknowledgments

Sniglets: Reprinted with permission of Macmillan Publishing Company from *When Sniglets Ruled the Earth* by Rich Hall. Copyright © 1989 by Not the Network Company, Inc.

We would like to thank the following teachers for their helpful and practical suggestions: Sandra Forkins of the Ridgeland School District in Oak Lawn, Illinois, Bonnie Koontz from St. Joan of Arc School in Toledo, Ohio, and Theresa Wilkie from the Hinsdale School District in Hinsdale, Illinois, and to Theresa Zigmond for editing the original edition of **Open**.

Also, we appreciate Kathy Kupka for proofreading this edition and Joe Koziarski for his illustrations.

ISBN 0-933282-07-9   paperback
ISBN 0-933282-09-5   hardbound

Copyright, Stack the Deck, Inc, © 1999, 1991, 1985 Revised Edition

Tips to Improve Use of *Open the Deck*

A. Success depends upon active teacher involvement. Be enthusiastic. Develop a positive attitude with your students.

B. When in doubt--**model**. Make no assumptions.

C. Be sure to preview this **Teacher's Guide** for advance suggestions with each unit.

D. Don't be afraid to **modify**. Adjust to students' needs.

E. **Quality**, not quantity, should be more important.

F. Consider a 60/40 target for use of *Open the Deck*. Use *Open the Deck* as the writing text for 60% of your time, teaching the *writer's vocabulary* through sentence manipulation and *the writing process*, emphasizing grading sheets(scoring rubrics, student think sheets, checklist sheets, and especially our **sentence opening sheet**. The other 40% could be devoted to other writing projects, e.g., Donald Graves' *Writer's Workshop*, seasonal assignments, responding to literature, writing across the curriculum topics, etc.

G. When working with a new concept or tool, things often get **worse** before they get **better**.

If you are interested in receiving information about our writing workshops, computer software programs, writing folders or other books in our series, write to The Stack the Deck Writing Program, P.O. Box 429, Tinley Park, IL 60477 or call toll free-**1-800-253-5737** or e-mail us at staff@stackthedeck.com. Visit our web site: **www.stackthedeck.com**.

TABLE OF CONTENTS

In the **Stack the Deck Writing Program**, the writing process is taught. The next few pages explain our process and highlight some of the teacher labor-saving devices incorporated in our writing system. Please refer to these pages every time you begin to teach the **Major Writing Assignment** in each unit.

All major writing assignments follow the process approach. This is the **four step procedure** modeled from professional authors. It has gained wide-spread popularity due to its success in improving student writing.

1. Prewriting: any activity or experience that readies students to write. Prewriting, before the actual writing occurs, can be reading a story, listening to a speaker, taking a field trip, drawing a picture, watching a video, visiting a web site, etc. Prewriting is intended to accomplish two objectives: 1) give the student a topic to write about, and 2) give the student information with which to write. *NOTE: You are also urged to encourage students to select their own topics occasionally. They then must do more independent prewriting. A balance between teacher-given and student-chosen topics is desirable.*

2. Drafting: the recording of ideas from prewriting. Drafting is a first try, and it's often in a rough form. The concern is with the flow of ideas, not with perfect form, spelling, punctuation, or neatness. Drafting should be quick and uninterrupted.

3. Rewriting and Proofreading: changing a draft to improve it. Rewriting deals with content improvement (ideas, organization, vocabulary); proofreading deals with mechanics (correct spelling, punctuation, grammar).

4. Publishing: the public sharing of polished writing. Publishing can take many forms: posting papers in the classroom or elsewhere in the school; oral presentations to partners, whole class, or other classrooms; printing the paper in a newsletter, class newspaper, student publication, or making a book. Publishing accomplishes two objectives: 1) it rewards the hard work in the first three steps, and 2) it motivates careful work due to the expanded audience.

The Stack the Deck Writing Process

STAGE ONE: PREWRITING

Student Objectives and Evaluation Sheet--Rubric (Labor-Saving Device #1)

All major writing assignments in *Open the Deck* include a **Student Objectives and Evaluation Sheet (SOES)**. They are found in the back of this **Teacher's Guide**. The SOES sheets--rubrics-- are designed to be used as a grading sheet when evaluating student writing.

Each **SOES** sheet or grading sheet (scoring rubric) lists the key student objectives or the assignment. Students should be given a copy of this sheet at the **end** of the prewriting stage or at the beginning of the writing stage of the process approach. This will remind them of what the assignment is stressing before they begin to write.

Of course, you may modify the sheet or design your own.

The **overall effect of the paper** objective allows the teacher to be somewhat *subjective*. We call this the **teacher stroke objective**. It allows the teacher to give the student extra points for incorporating a recent vocabulary word or experimenting with a different structure. It is used for positive reinforcement. It is the "brownie point" objective. The choice is yours. ***Students love it!*

Think Sheet (Labor-Saving Device #2)

A **Think Sheet** is provided for each major writing assignment to help students generate ideas before writing. Students should save their **Think Sheets** to refer to when they are ready to write the first draft. **Think Sheets** help students to stay focused on the topic and to support their ideas with specific details. (**Stage Two**)

STAGE TWO: WRITING THE FIRST DRAFT

Here are three good rules for writing a first draft:

1. If you can't spell a word, sound it out the best you can and circle it to check later. This if referred to as inventive spelling. It allows the flow of ideas.

2. If your handwriting is not your neatest, that's **OK**. You can clean it up later. First drafts need only be legible enough to read back later.

3. If you have trouble writing a part of your story, don't worry. You can work on it later. This takes the pressure off, and it allows the flow of ideas.

To facilitate rewriting (stage three), students should:

- write in pencil
- skip every other line (Note: To help students remember, have them (✔)
- alternate lines in the margin.) See the example below:
- number each sentence after the draft is finished

Drafting on a Computer

Students should be given the option of drafting on a computer with a word processor program if:

    * they can keyboard at least as fast as they handwrite
    * computers are available to them for an adequate amount of time

0		
	✔	
	✔	
	✔	
	✔	

Some teachers like to prepare a wall chart that reminds students how to write a first draft.

> **Guess and Go Spelling**
>
> **Write Quickly**
>
> **Not Perfect**
>
> **In Pencil**
>
> **Skip lines**
>
> **Number sentences**
>
> **Using Front Side of Paper Only**

STAGE THREE: REWRITING

There are two parts to this stage of the writing process:

* revision -- improving content (ideas, organization, vocabulary, sentence flow)
* proofreading -- fixing errors (spelling, mechanics, handwriting)

It is far more difficult to teach students how to revise than to proofread, and you already know how difficult it can be just to teach proofreading skills. Both kinds of rewriting are taught in this book.

If students realize the rough draft is just a first try, then altering it won't seem so destructive to the hard work put in. The term *sloppy copy* comes from poet Ingrid Wendt: it reinforces the notion of a temporary draft. So does the term *messify*, which was coined by Donald Graves, the main popularizer of the process approach to writing in the elementary schools.

Rewriting Alone

When students read back their compositions, they should be encouraged to read aloud softly to hear their voice. All writers have a distinctive voice: the unique quality of individual expression. Just as each student has a unique speaking voice, so does each have a unique writing voice. Oral reading allows students to hear their writing voices. Many times students will see or hear something that needs fixing and catch it right there.

Sentence Opening Sheet (Labor-Saving Device #3)

Our **most lauded teacher labor-saving device** is the **Sentence Opening Sheet**. It is introduced on pages 40 & 42 in **Unit 2** of the student text and explained in detail.

Rewriting with Help--Conferencing

The rewriting technique of listening to your students read to you is known as **conferencing.** Have one student at a time read you her draft. You sit across a table from her listening. Do not try to look at the draft -- you do not want to see any spelling errors, misplaced commas, sloppy handwriting, etc. All you are interested in is the content. Listen to the draft carefully just as you would if the student was orally telling you a story about what happened to her over the weekend.

When she is finished reading, do the following:
* tell her what you especially liked about the story. Maybe an unusual word, name, or an interesting phrase was terrific. Try to remember it, so you can quote it back to her.
* ask her how she feels generally about the story at this point. She may or may not ask for help.

* ask her a specific question about a confusing part in the story. Just as she could lose you while telling you about last weekend, she may be unclear in her writing. (However, if the story is acceptably clear and complete, congratulate her and call the next student.)
* If the student still needs help, ask her what she is planning on doing next with the story. Hopefully, she will commit to improving the confusing part you identified. This is her choice: it must be optional to maintain the author's ownership. She then returns to her desk to rewrite the rough part(s).

The above conference procedure was influenced by Donald Graves (*Writing: Teachers and Students at Work*), Lucy Calkins (*Lessons from a Child*), Keith Wetzel and Randy Boone (University of Oregon's Department of Computers and Technology in Education).

A Classroom management note: When you are in a conference with a student, the rest of the class must be busy so that you are not interrupted. You will need utmost concentration to accomplish the 4 points above. Teach the class that no interruptions will be tolerated. Establish rules so that other students do not interrupt a conference, e.g, ask a classmate for help instead of the teacher, write your name on the board if you need help soon, draw a picture of your story when you finished writing, etc.

To help students deal with errors in mechanics (punctuation, capitalization, spelling, handwriting), try some of these techniques:

* schedule a **second conference** to work with students individually on mechanical errors (difficult with time crunch).

* arrange for a **volunteer** to be in the classroom during writing time. This could be a parent, a university student working toward credit, a student tutor from a nearby middle or high school, or a student aide from a higher grade in your school. Any of the above volunteers would only be responsible for helping with errors you want covered; train them before-hand.

* assign proofreading partners and supply a checklist of items to help. (See below.)

Rewriting with Help--Checklist Sheet (Labor-Saving Device #4)

Each assignment includes a **Checklist Sheet**. A common use of the **Checklist** is to have students exchange papers using this sheet as a guide as they cross-evaluate each other's papers. We strongly recommend that you model with your students how to use a **Checklist** for the first assignment in **Open the Deck**.

When your students use the **Checklist Sheet** in the peer evaluation, you might want to assign each member of the group (cooperative learning teams) specific responsibilities. Student 1 can concentrate on items 1-4, student 2, items 5-7; student 3, items 8-10; and so on.

SPECIAL SPELLING NOTE: Spelling is an important mechanics skill--kids and parents both identify correct spelling as *good writing*. While other aspects of writing are more important, it's true that correct spelling is very important to the reader.

Here are some techniques to help students spell correctly for the final copy.

*   **Franklin Spelling Ace:** this is a battery-operated mini-computer (3 x 6) that has 80,000 words in its memory. The user types in her spelling of a word, and the Spelling Ace compares it to its dictionary entries. It costs around $60-70 and can be placed at a Learning Center for independent use during Rewriting. It is very effective at identifying the correct spelling.

*   personal dictionaries: students can keep a running list of troublesome words so that they can refer to it before asking for help.

*   whole-group mini-lessons: if a word is misspelled in many student drafts, teach it to the whole class. Draw attention to any rule they may follow (e.g., *running* doubles the consonant) or any useful related words (e.g., *lonesome* is related to *alone* and *lonely*.)

Rewriting on a Computer

If students have a draft entered into a computer and saved onto a disk, they should be given the opportunity to revise with a word processor program. Word processing is a great motivator for all writers who dislike rewriting: it is fast, clean, and fun to insert, delete, move, and find/replace. Rewriting on a computer requires:

*   keyboarding skill
*   knowledge of the word processor's functions and key commands
*   adequate time availability

STAGE FOUR: PUBLISHING

This is the public sharing of written work, and it is very important because it:

*   expands the audience beyond just the teacher
*   motivates careful rewriting through pride in ownership
*   rewards hard work during the other steps of the process

Publishing on a Computer

A printed hard copy of the story looks great. Access to *Page Maker* or *Newsroom* programs are also terrific, but require time to learn.

If you have access to a graphics software program, let the students create designs or illustrations on the computer to enrich their finished products.

STUDENT LEARNING OBJECTIVES

1. The student will use the same word with different functions.
2. The student will create sentences using a language machine.
3. The student will break down sentences into kernel ideas.
4. The student will combine sentences with colorful kernels.
5. The student will punctuate a series of words or ideas correctly.
6. The student will expand using journalistic questions.
7. The student will write a short observation of a scene.
8. The student will complete a **Think Sheet**.
9. The student will critique a composition using a **Checklist Sheet**.

ORAL LANGUAGE INTO WRITING

We begin each unit with oral language activities to build student confidence. These activities are designed to assist students in discovering how much they already know about their language. By heightening this awareness, confidence with using the language will increase. The learning of new writing skills later in the book should come easier as a result.

One major discovery the students will make is that our language is extremely *flexible*. The infinite number of ways to express a single thought or idea requires the teacher to expect more than one correct answer for some exercises. Therefore, this teacher guide will provide suggested, or possible answers with the understanding that others may be just as good, or even better. Be flexible!! Encourage creative responses!!

The tone of the oral language warm-ups should be light and playful. The intent is for students to enjoy manipulating their language in the exercises. A positive attitude from the teacher will greatly help to set a positive mood for use of the rest of the book.

FUNCTIONAL SHIFT, page 2

If you feel your students need more of an explanation regarding form and function, you may want to give them the help they need before you start any of the activities that follow. By truly understanding the concepts of form and function first, their confidence will grow with each activity.

WARM-UP ACTIVITY 1, page 2

Ask students to think of other uses for **bake**. Here are some additional uses from Theresa Wilkie, a teacher at Hinsdale Jr. High School in Hinsdale, Illinois.

baked to a crisp	Baker's Chocolate	baking powder
Baker's Square	baked potato	sunbaked skin

WARM-UP ACTIVITY 2, page 2

Be sure and have some resulting examples shared orally with the entire class. The more students can **hear** the function of different words, the more they will enjoy this activity.

WARM-UP ACTIVITY 3, page 3

The students should have some **fun** with the possible combinations. Try some **orally** with the class as a warm-up. Call out the column numbers for them to try. Then give them a photocopy of page 3, so they can write their answers in the blanks. You might also want to make a transparency and conduct this activity as a class project. Note that verbs in column 2 may need new endings.

1. Katie cooks the frozen vegetables.
2. Jenny cuts some boiled cakes.
3. Bernie eggs Lisa's scrambled potatoes.
4. Jenny fries Katie!
5. Lisa boils, fries, and bakes frozen vegetables.
6. Jenny cooks a scrambled potato, but Katie bakes two pounded eggs.
7. Boiling some scrambled cakes, Katie cut two pounded vegetables.
8. A potato was fried by Bernie.

SENTENCE MANIPULATION

Getting Started with Sentence Combining

The heart of **The Stack the Deck Writing Program** is teaching four sentence manipulatory skills--*combining, rearranging, subtracting,* and *expanding.* Mastery of these skills will not only improve your students' syntactic fluency but also provide them with a writer's vocabulary that will aid them in revising a composition.

Before you begin the first sentence-combining exercise in *Open the Deck*, we suggest that you write four sentences like these on the blackboard or overhead projector transparency:

> There is a boy.
> The boy is small.
> There is a pond.
> The boy fell.

Ask your students to make one sentence out of these four as quickly as possible--*orally.* Automatically, someone will probably say:

> The small boy fell into the pond.
> *or*
> There is a small boy who fell into the pond.

As soon as you hear a response, bring out a cauliflower or a cabbage or a grapefruit, and tell your students that they are actually looking at a brain. Better yet, don a **brain thinking cap** or bring out a **brain jello mold** and tell your students that the greatest computer in the world--their brain-- automatically composed one sentence using special skills:

Combining	They combined four sentences into one.
Rearranging	They rearranged words, putting *small* before *pond*.
Subtracting	They subtracted unnecessary words.
Expanding	They expanded, adding *into* or *who*.

These **writer's vocabulary** words become revision words as your students begin to rewrite a first draft. Here are some questions you can ask them as they study their first drafts--sloppy copies:

Combining:

1. Do you repeat the same dull openings, e. g., I, The, And then, etc.?
2. Which sentences can you combine to make them more interesting for your audience?

Rearranging

1. Which sentences can I rearrange to avoid repeating the same dull sentence beginnings?
2. Am I emphasizing key ideas by placing them in a position of importance-- beginning or end of a sentence? If not, how can I rearrange the sentence?

Subtracting

1. Where did I pad my sentences by adding empty or dead words to fill up space?
2. Did I get off the topic? Where should I subtract unnecessary words or ideas?

Expanding

1. Where do I need to expand with journalistic questions--Who? What? When? Where? How? Why?--to support my main ideas.
2. Did I skip information my audience needs to know? Where should I expand?

Our **Learning Off-the-Wall Classroom Posters** serve as a constant reminder of our writer's vocabulary and can be used to reinforce key ideas taught in our textbooks.

Also, our most lauded teacher labor saving device, the **Sentence Opening Sheet**, helps students apply the skills of combining and rearranging in revising a composition. We begin the sentence manipulation activities by emphasizing that sentences can be broken into separate *kernels* of information. Students are then shown that these kernels are combined in many different ways to create sentences with more variety.

Initially, the students work on identifying the kernels of sentences in **EXERCISE 1.**
Quickly, however, they move to **EXERCISE 2** where the real fun begins. Students now
practice combining kernels in order to *stretch* sentences so that they contain more
information, which is also packaged in a more colorful manner. The emphasis is on
expanding sentences, and it is carried through in **EXERCISES 2-8.**

BREAKING DOWN SENTENCES INTO KERNELS, page 4

We normally do not think in sentence form, but for the purpose of finding all the
kernels, we want to drill with *There is . . .*

EXERCISE 1, page 4   **POSSIBLE ANSWERS**

1. a. There is a dog.
    b. The dog is yours.
    c. The dog wears.
    d. There are boots.
    e. The boots are navy blue.
    f. The boots are from the army.
    g. There are suspenders.
    h. The suspenders are orange.

2. a. There is a vampire.
    b. The vampire is evil.
    c. The vampire swooped.
    d. There was a maiden.
    e. The maiden was lovely.
    f. The maiden was young.

3. a. There is a troll.
    b. The troll has whiskers.
    c. The whiskers are green.
    d. The troll lived.
    e. There is a bridge.
    f. The bridge is creaky.

4. a. There is someone named Slim Sampson.
    b. Slim Sampson slipped.
    c. Slim Sampson snickered.
    d. There is a corner.

5. a. There is someone named Wilma.
    b. Wilma is wild.
    c. Wild Wilma waltzed.
    d. There is a sprinkler.
    e. The sprinkler sprinkles water.
    f. The sprinkler is whirling.

COMBINING WITH COLORFUL KERNELS, page 5

This exercise may be done orally and/or a few sentences written, depending on the needs of your students.

EXERCISE 2, pages 5-6   **POSSIBLE ANSWERS**

1. My brawny, little brother, Seymour, washed his hands in Jell-O.
2. Wally skied warily down the scary mountain.
3. Georgianna yawned, grunted, and scratched her itchy head.
4. The rugged wind surfer twisted his board across the wake.
5. The scrawny trapeze artist happily caught her huge husband.
6. Leroy wore leopard-spotted tights in the crazy, funny play.
7. The slobbery pig ate fat, juicy grasshoppers.
8. Professor U. R. A. Grouch had a hooked nose like a fierce hawk.
9. Ulysses won the squealing pig contest, squealing like Miss Piggy.
                or
    Squealing like Miss Piggy, Ulysses won the squealing pig contest.
10. My muscular Uncle Herb rides his exercise bike.

EXPANDING IDEAS USING JOURNALISTIC QUESTIONS, page 6

Give a brief introduction of the importance of providing support for ideas in writing. One way to achieve this goal is to use the journalistic questions to expand.

EXERCISE 4, page 8

Why not make a transparency of this exercise and have your students complete the first few as a class project? After the students expand with the journalistic questions, you might want them to rearrange some sentences to begin with a different opening. Even though the rearranging skill will be introduced later in *Open the Deck*, it doesn't hurt to emphasize it, especially if you have one of our **Writer's Vocabulary** posters in your classroom.

The answers will vary for this exercise. Here are some students' sentences for numbers 1 and 2 in Exercise 4.

1. The fragile ice in the middle of the pond cracked because the snowmobile was too heavy.
2. As soon as she stepped on the ice, the figure skater fell because she had put on roller skates instead of ice skates.

NOTE: Other answers will vary. Encourage sharing. Again, be sure to have some students share orally.

EXERCISE 5, page 9

Make sure that you work on the board with the entire class when introducing these items. Students should enjoy this sharing, and it will help you monitor their early progress.

You might also want to make this a cooperative learning activity by having the various groups in your class work on individual sets of sentences. Obviously answers will vary greatly for this activity.

WORD STORAGE BANK, page 9

This Word Storage Bank lends itself to many different assignments, classroom activities, and bulletin board ideas. Make it work for you and your students. Each student could have a chance to contribute.

For example, some student(s) may volunteer to draw a *bank* on poster board or art paper. This can be used for a bulletin board display on which students could *deposit* new words. They would *gain interest* whenever they used a new word from the bank in their sentences.

Since this bank chart would always be in view, hopefully it would prod the students to incorporate the new words not only in their assignments but also as a part of their everyday vocabulary.

PUTTING IT ALL TOGETHER, pages 9-11

EXERCISE 6, page 11

With this exercise, students will have many sentence parts to manipulate into new, more creative sentences. Be sure to share some of the examples orally with the entire class. Also be sure to use this exercise to link to an understanding of two of the writer's vocabulary words students have just learned--combining and expanding. Ask students to identify sentences of their own where they have applied these techniques.

AN EASY COMPOSING RULE

EXERCISE 7, page 12   **POSSIBLE ANSWERS**

1. Leon, the elephant, wears old, smelly socks.
2. We gave my sister pale pink, delicate, friendly jellyfish.
3. The wolf's pointed, yellow teeth glistened in the moonlight.
4. Larry trains small, lively, hungry alligators.
5. His brand new, red, cross-country skis were in the closet.

Encourage your students to experiment with a different structure instead of always following the pattern in the book. Here is are examples for sentences 3 and 4.

3. The wolf's teeth, which were yellow and pointed, glistened in the moonlight.

4. Larry trains small, lively alligators, and they are also very hungry.

Although these structures do not follow the pattern sample, they exhibit good use of new structures and are acceptable--as long as all kernels have been used. Remember, language confidence and manipulation, not similarity, is the goal!

COMMA RULE 1, page 13

One of the key ingredients in **The Stack the Deck Writing Program** is teaching functional mechanics. Since students will be practicing combining sentences using a series of adjectives, this is a perfect time to discuss punctuating a series of items. (You may want to address the ambiguity of the rule since there is a lot of confusion as to whether or not a comma is used before an **and**. Example: His brief case was scuffed, bruised, smashed, **and** perfectly practical. Since both methods are correct, we think application of the rule here is the easiest for younger students to remember.)

EXERCISE 8, page 13

Be sure to ask students to read their *best* sentences. Students may also pick their favorite sentence, write it on one sheet of poster paper, and then illustrate it. This would be a good bulletin board for showing off student creativity.

PUNCTUATION RULES FOR YOUR NOTEBOOK, page 13

The text recommends that you have students set aside some portion of their notebook for collecting punctuation rules. This can be quite handy for a quick reference. You may also want to consider laminating a large chart for the front of the classroom and writing each rule as it is covered. This serves as a constant visual reminder for students as well.

USING WRITING TRAITS TO IMPROVE YOUR COMPOSITION, page 14

Feel free to modify this list to match your district or state. If the terms "trait" or "criteria" are elusive to your students, try "quality" or "characteristic."

Because so many state and national writing assessments now emphasize mastery of certain writing techniques or skills, we wanted to provide students with practice related to these characteristics. the six skills or "traits" emphasized in this book are : ideas, organization, voice, word choice, sentence fluency, and conventions. The terms or categories use in your area may be slightly different, but these should be lots of similarities. Adapt if you need or want to.

On the Spot Reporter

> Review **The Stack the Deck Writing Process** on pages 4-9 in this guide before teaching this assignment.

STAGE ONE: PREWRITING, page 15

STUDENT OBJECTIVE AND EVALUATION SHEET--SCORING RUBRIC

See **page 61** in this guide for a copy of the grading sheet.

Exercise 9, page 15

This activity provides some focus awareness of the trait "word choice." Students use a structure paragraph to try out some new vivid adjectives, verbs, similes, etc.. Be sure that students both fill in the blanks and replace the bold words. Share orally or on an overhead.

THINK SHEET, pages 18-19

The **Think Sheet** is obviously intended as a tool for collecting as many ideas as possible. As this is the first **Think Sheet** in the text, it is important to introduce it well. Students need to know that a slap-dash method of completion is not the best approach.

Modeling is probably the best way to insure success. Consider doing **numbers 1** and **2** with the entire class as a means to demonstrate just how many good details can be included. Have each student do these items on their own and then complete **numbers 1** and **2** as a model with the entire class. Ask for oral examples as you go.

Once you've established a pattern of thoroughness with these first two examples, allow students to complete the entire **Think Sheet** on their own. Here is an example student model from a middle school student. Note how the ideas on the **Think Sheet** enabled him to stay focused on the prompt and support his ideas with specific details.

Sometimes teachers like to use real student models of writing to help "prime the pump" before students begin their think sheet or first draft. For example, the teacher could use this student draft and have students work backwards to create the think sheet that might have been used to write this. Many teachers choose not to use models because they don't want sway or influence student imitation. This is fine, too. Do what is most comfortable for you.

"Santa" Saves the Day

One day in early December, with Christmas rapidly approaching, I was at Best Buy (a large video and electronics store) looking for another item for my Christmas list. The place was seething with people. The store was peppered with flashing Christmas lights and red and green decorations. Kids were dragging around their parents to show them their choices and whining when they were told no. The grownups were groaning over the price of things while trying to keep up with their kids.

The owner and employees were just as busy. The owner was dressed up as Santa and the line was half the length of the store. Employees were listening to price complaints, helping people finds things, and collecting huge amounts of money. It was the perfect time for a robbery.

I wouldn't have notice the robbers if I didn't bump into one. They had entered nonchalantly, without attracting much attention. They pretended to look at some of the videos, but they were really working their way over to the cash registers. I wouldn't have given it second thought if it weren't for their appearance. The three of them were all tall and fairly meaty, maybe 6'2" and at least 220 pounds each. They all had long hair and hats hiding their faces. Their shirts were torn and they were covered with nasty scars.

The strange men worked their way behind the cash registers and one pulled out a gun. Once the crowd realized what was happening, chaos broke out. I dived in an aisle and peeked around the corner. Everyone was fighting to get a safe spot. One man dove into a game rack so hard he started bleeding. The robbers looked as if they were in complete control.

"Nobody try anything and this cashier will live to see another day," one robber growled with a gun to the cashier's head.

Then I noticed Santa (the owner) sneaking cautiously up to the man with the gun. He had a video rack above his head and was waving it around menacingly. He hit the man with a glancing blow and grabbed the gun. The men ran away before the police arrived.

Afterwards, the customers were still shaky, but Santa was even worse because his store was a disaster. The customers had managed to knock down almost every display and merchandise rack in the store. Santa was barking out orders to everyone, even the customers that were still hanging around. It'll be a long night for the janitors!

STAGE TWO: WRITING THE FIRST DRAFT, page 20

Suggestions for drafting are quite complete in the student text. Do be sure, however, that you review and discuss all the information on pages 20 and 21.

STAGE THREE: REWRITING, page 22

When beginning the **REVISION** process in *Open the Deck*, it's also not a bad time to reinforce the standards you will be expecting during the grading process. This way, your expectations are not a mystery, and they can be helpful as students begin final modifications. Consider reviewing the **STUDENT OBJECTIVES AND EVALUATION SHEETS-rubrics--** found on pages 61-68 in this guide.

ON THE SPOT REPORTER CHECKLIST, page 23

An excellent way to model the use of this **Checklist** is to model using two student volunteers in front of the class, (or a student and the teacher). Work with this pair, if possible, ahead of time so that all the key ingredients are demonstrated. These would be: 1) using the 12 inch voice, 2) reading papers first aloud to each other and then on your own, 3) including adequate feedback on the sheet, and 4) proper listening and on-task behavior.

Have the **Checklists** filled out ahead of time and done on an overhead. This will save time and allow the proper format to be shared with the entire class.

STAGE FOUR: PUBLISHING, page 24

Theresa Wilkie took the assignment *one step further* and offered this publishing suggestion:

Read 3-5 papers the class has voted to be the best.
Ask a juvenile officer and/or reporter for the police beat to attend class.
Ask the officer to respond to content of plot and probability.
Ask the reporter to do the same while commenting on the craft of the writing.

Community involvement: If the officer and reporter attend the class on the same day, perhaps a feature including the *best* paper could be printed in the local news.

A number of ensuing discussions could take place once the students start reading their robbery descriptions. Which descriptions sound as if they could really happen? Which one has the most twists in the plot? Which one has the most universal appeal?

COMBINING

STUDENT LEARNING OBJECTIVES

1. The student will discuss and create never heard before sentences.
2. The student will combine sentences with glue words (subordinating conjunctions).
3. The student will vary his/her sentence openings.
4. The student will punctuate dependent clauses correctly.
5. The student will discuss the differences in meaning in sentences because of subordinating conjunctions.
6. The student will combine sentences into a paragraph using subordinating conjunctions **(Glue Words)**.
7. The student will revise a composition using a **Sentence Opening Sheet**.
8. The student will compose a composition using all the sentence skills he/she has been taught.

ORAL LANGUAGE INTO WRITING

NEVER HEARD BEFORE SENTENCES, page 25

WARM-UP ACTIVITY 1, page 25

This light-hearted activity is designed to enforce the idea of language acquisition: your students already have advance language ability.

WARM-UP ACTIVITY 2, page 25

You might need to remind the class that humor has its boundaries in a school, i. e., to consider appropriateness.

SENTENCE MANIPULATION

Unit 2 introduces **glue words** (subordinating conjunctions) as another way of combining sentences. This combining strategy is modeled for students to show how they can effectively join shorter sentences together. Both the functional name (glue words) and the formal grammatical name (subordinating conjunctions), are used in the text. Teachers may stress either type of name, or both, depending on personal preference.

The list, or collection, of glue words found in the text is not exhaustive. The list contains the words used most often and should be sufficient for completion of the exercises. If the teacher or a student wants to add to the list, he or she should do so. **NOTE:** A wall poster for each family of words is very helpful to students. For example, make a poster in the shape of a glue bottle with glue words from page 26 on it.

Because of the flexibility of our language, many possible sentence combinations result for each exercise in this unit. Accept other answers if they make sense. Encourage students to try the less commonly used glue words (instead of *because)* each time.

EXERCISE 1, pages 26-27

Here is a list of **glue words** that could be used to combine the sentence sets in this exercise.

1. after, because, since, when, whenever, while
2. because, since, when, while, after
3. even though, since
4. although, because, even though, since
5. in order that, so that
6. after, because, before, when
7. after, as long as, because, if, since, when, whenever, where, wherever, while
8. as long as, as if, as though, because, if, when, whenever, while
9. because, as long as, since
10. although, even though, though
11. because, since
12. after, although, before, even though, though, until
13. although, even though
14. as, as long as, because, after, before, even though, since, though, when, whenever, where, wherever, while
15. as if, as though (Note: This is a difficult one.)

VARYING SENTENCE OPENINGS WITH GLUE WORDS, page 27

EXERCISE 2, pages 28-29

Possible Answers.

1. Although...postponed, Dawn...
2. When Jay...job, he...
3. After Dora...oysters, she...
4. Before Santa...chimney,...Jenny...
5. So that everyone...prize, I...
6. Wherever Donna goes, I...
7. Since Aretha...quick, she...
8. If the...dirty, Cousin...
9. As the...sings, the...
10. Where the...place, Main...
11. Because the...weak, the...
12. Even though Nancy...broke, she...
13. Before the...web, the...
14. Whenever Christine is hungry, she...

MORE PRACTICE COMBINING WITH GLUE WORDS, page 29

EXERCISE 3, pages 29-30

All possible **glue words** should be used at least once. Review the comma rule before your students begin this exercise.

1. Before the four o'clock Thursday game, the umpire rubbed up the baseballs.
2. After she eats breakfast, Meg brushes her teeth in the bathroom.
3. When Jake passed his science exam, Jake (or *he*) was promoted to eighth grade.
4. As the concert was in progress, the fans rocked in their stadium seats.
5. While the wind blew, it stirred up the dust on the field.

6. When Allan moved to a new apartment, Allan (or *he*) rented a U-Haul trailer.
7. After she went to many used car lots, Niki bought a 1968 Volkswagen car.
8. Until the terrifying storm ended, Lucas and Madi waited in the barn.
9. Since Aileen washed the pots and pans in the kitchen, Paul emptied the dishwasher.
10. After Bo retrieved the torn ball, he dropped it at his master's feet.

UNCOMBINING SENTENCES, page 31

EXERCISE 4, page 31

2a. We recycle glass.	4a. Cindra will help build the fort.
2b. We still have too much garbage.	4b. Kendra finds the hammer and saw.
3a. It rains.	5a. Her party was excellent.
3b. It pours.	5b. The birthday cake fell onto the floor.

COMBINING AND EXPANDING IDEAS INTO A PARAGRAPH, page 31

Some students still have difficulty understanding these glue words because of sequence, time order, and cause and effect. If your students need a quick review, this might be the best time for it.

EXERCISE 5, page 32

If you decide on cooperative learning, be sure to clearly state the procedure, rules, and expectations. Allow for class-sharing of finished drafts. Remind them to skip lines, circle unknown spelling, and go for the flow.

CHANGING MEANINGS BY POSITIONING GLUE WORDS, page 33

EXTENSION ACTIVITY: Theresa Wilkie from Hinsdale Jr. High in Hinsdale, Illinois, suggests:

For added fun have the students watch you change the meaning of a sentence by *only* moving the word *only*. Use the chalkboard or transparency for all to see.

> She broke her arm.
> Only she broke her arm.
> She only broke her arm.
> She broke only her arm.
> She broke her only arm.
> She broke her arm only.

EXERCISE 6, page 33

Discuss the different meanings. This exercise should be a whole class oral activity.

EXERCISE 7, page 34

Complete this as an oral activity. If your students begin their rearranged sentence with a dependent clause, remind them of the proper punctuation.

MAJOR WRITING ASSIGNMENT

Review **The Stack the Deck Writing Process** on pages 4-9 in this guide before teaching this assignment.

STAGE ONE: PREWRITING, page 35

STUDENT OBJECTIVES AND EVALUATION SHEET

See **page 62** in this guide for a copy of the grading sheet.

WRITING TRAITS

Notice another writing trait, sentence fluency, is introduced here. Emphasize that good writing has its own rhythm. As a new writing trait is introduced, you might want to list them on a chart in front of the classroom.

WRITING PROMPT, page 36

Because of the latitude involved in this exercise, students may find it a little more difficult. Some students may even need a review of baseball. You may want to get students started by working on the board. Or you may think it necessary to use the entire exercise as a **class project**, then allow students to write individual endings. You be the judge of your students' comfort level. Whatever the case, individual stories should be shared orally in class.

The subject of this assignment is an imaginary fictional story about a baseball player. As with **The Colfax Crushers** story earlier in this unit, the kernel sentences are given to students. This time, however, each student works independently to rewrite the story by combining the little sentences into longer, more interesting ones. They now have three combining strategies. Also, students need to create an ending.

THINK SHEET, page 37

As always, the prewriting stage includes a planning sheet. By deciding beforehand on combining strategies, Stage Two will move more smoothly.

STAGE TWO: WRITING THE FIRST DRAFT, page 38

Drafting Rules, page 38

Remind students that skipping lines and writing in pencil will facilitate Stage Three.

STAGE THREE: REWRITING, page 38

USING THE SENTENCE OPENING SHEET TO REVISE, page 38

Since independent revision is a goal for all young writers, the **SOS** is provided as a tool to learn how to revise a draft. Column 1 should be familiar from earlier in this unit. Column 3 is now added: **Verbs. Jan's Chance** is written entirely in present tense, so any verbs added by students also must be present tense (DOES). Column 4 is skipped for now to keep things simple. Of course, you may assign it if you desire.

EXERCISE 8, pages 39-40 **The Colfax Crushers**

This exercise introduces the **Sentence Opening Sheet (SOS)**, a handy proofreading device. Each of the four columns is designed to call attention to likely problem areas which may appear in the students' writing. Every sentence is analyzed. *Permission is granted to reproduce the SOS form for your students.* The teacher may want to use an overhead transparency to demonstrate; students can write on their own individual copies which have been photocopied.

This class project can be accomplished by students' suggesting combinations to the teacher, who records them either on the chalkboard or overhead projector. (Give students some time to read and plan combinations before beginning.) **Skipping lines and numbering each new sentence is also helpful.** It is important to demonstrate skipping lines and numbering sentences because in all written assignments which follow, students will be instructed to do the same. Some teachers have found it helpful to have students use colored highlighters to color code those sentences which they will combine. Minor changes in the story in the form of additional words, deletions, and substitutions are acceptable. The order of sentences may also be changed. **NOTE:** Set this rule: No more than 2 *ands* per sentence.

At the beginning, an **SOS** can be confusing to students, so only the first and fourth columns will be introduced initially; columns 2 and 3 will be introduced later.

The purpose of column one, **Sentence Openings** (first four words), is to call attention to varied (or redundant) sentence beginnings. This matter is an important stylistic consideration; column one makes the writer see it. In fact, some professional authors employ this technique in order to get a complete view of all their sentence openings of a particular piece.

The fourth column, **# of words**, is used to help writers see if they have written short, choppy sentences, varied their sentence lengths, or written overly long sentences, possibly resulting in run-ons.

Here is a sample of a possible way to execute **EXERCISE 8**. Notice that the original 28 sentences are combined into 10 longer sentences. Notice the different sentence beginnings.

The Colfax Crushers

1. The tall, scrawny quarterback at Colfax Middle School was in seventh grade. **2.** Because he wasn't very good, his wobbly passes were constantly intercepted when he threw them. **3.** Whenever he tried to run the ball, he was sacked, as he had a weak line. **4.** As long as his team lost so pitifully, he was teased. **5.** In the summer, the quarterback worried about the next season. **6.** In order to put on weight, he worked out and drank thirty-two milk shakes a day. **7.** As he rode his bike, he looked hard for strong, big, fast guys who had just been promoted. **8.** Things were much better in the fall because he had found plenty of help. **9.** The points piled up because the team the quarterback recruited beat everyone. **10.** They were known as **The Colfax Crushers**.

SENTENCE OPENING (first four words)	GLUE SPECIAL	DID VERBS	# OF WORDS
1. The tall, scrawny quarterback			11
2. Because he wasn't very			15
3. Whenever he tried to			16
4. As long as his			11
5. In the summer the			9
6. In order to put			17
7. As he rode his			18
8. Things were much better			13
9. The points piled up			12
10. They were known as			8

Here is another sample group paper written by the 6th grade class at Monroe Middle School in Eugene, Oregon. See if your class can beat their five sentences. Send entries to us, and we'll publish it in one of our company's newsletter or on our web site.

The Colfax Crushers

1. The green, scrawny, seventh grade quarterback at Colfax Middle School wasn't very good because he had a weak line. **2.** Whenever he threw passes, they were intercepted, and whenever he ran the ball, he was sacked. **3.** Then he was teased because his team lost that summer. **4.** While the quarterback worried about next season, he worked out, he drank 32 milk shakes a day, he put on weight, and he rode his bike looking for big, strong, fast guys who had just been promoted, and he found help in the fall. **5.** Things were better because points were scored, and the team the quarterback recruited beat everyone, so from then on, they were known as **The Colfax Crushers**.

GETTING BY WITH A LITTLE HELP FROM MY FRIEND, page 44

We also want to teach young writers that assistance, advice, and feedback are desired by talented writers. Therefore, we provide a structured approach to peer editing: **The Partner Checklist**.

Decide on assigning partners or small groups. The former is more easily managed; the latter provides each student with multiple feedback. As always with cooperative learning activities, clearly state the objectives, the roles, the time allotted, expectations on behavior, and the means of evaluating their cooperation.

POLISHING UP YOUR FIRST DRAFT, page 46

Many young writers fail to see the need for rewriting their hard earned stories. Even when a peer, or group of peers, recommends changes, some students resist. This is a developmental issue: more mature, talented, confident writers accept criticism gladly in order to improve. So be gentle, but urge all students to seriously consider their partner's checklist advice.

STAGE FOUR: PUBLISHING, page 46

The baseball card is only a suggestion. If you like the idea, try it out. If not, think of another way to celebrate their completed stories.

Unit 3

SHOWING ACTION AND MOVEMENT

STUDENT LEARNING OBJECTIVES

1. The student will describe the same situation two times changing the tone for each set of sentences.
2. The student will combine sentences with **WH words** (relative pronouns).
3. The student will punctuate **WH** clauses correctly.
4. The student will combine sentences with **ING words** (verbals).
5. The student will punctuate **ING** phrases correctly.
6. The student will write a short paper which describes movement and action.
7. The student will organize the paper in a chronological sequence.
8. The student will support his ideas with specific details.

ORAL LANGUAGE INTO WRITING

CREATING DIFFERENT MOODS FOR YOUR AUDIENCE, page 47

WARM-UP ACTIVITY 1, pages 47

This activity is extremely powerful, but it can be a bit confusing for students. The best offense to avoid this confusion is class-directed modeling. Do number 1 with the entire class asking for ideas from various partners. Then the teacher has the option of sharing some different examples, using a different mood or tone, **OR**, you can again ask for examples from the class.

Be sure to share as many of the student examples as you can in an oral fashion.

SENTENCE MANIPULATION

The **SENTENCE MANIPULATION** tools which are introduced in this chapter should really help students beef up their writing repertoire. Most of the explanations in the student text are quite complete. However, you will want to review them ahead of time and provide your own direct comments during their introduction.

COMBINING WITH WH WORDS, page 49

This family of words is very useful to young writers because they can easily use them in their own writing.

EXERCISE 1, pages 50-51   POSSIBLE ANSWERS

1. Cheating, *which* is wrong, causes unfair grades.
         or
   Cheating, *which* causes unfair grades, is wrong.
2. The blazing fire, *which* started in the kitchen of the house, sent up black smoke.

3. Some odd people, *who* were demonstrating vacuum cleaners, stood at my door.
4. Ruta's Restaurant, *which* serves the best sauerkraut soup, is my favorite place for lunch.
5. The old shoe, *that* is torn, scuffed, and tongueless, belongs to Mrs. Hubbard.
6. Two alley cats, *who* fought all night, screeched like badly played violins.
7. Darin's pants, *which* are cutoff at the knees, keep his legs cool during the summer.
8. Your friend, *who* is Henry George Michael Carmichael, is playing the bugle.
9. The invitation, *which* arrived three weeks before the party, smelled like roses.
10. Jogging, *which* sometimes causes injuries, is heavy exercise.

COMMA RULE 3, page 51

Be sure and allow adequate time to discuss **WRITING RULE** 3 immediately after you finish **EXERCISE 1**. Students will have a good sense of the **FUNCTION** which precedes this introduction.

HIDDEN WORDS, page 52

EXERCISE 2, pages 52-53   POSSIBLE ANSWERS

1. Stanley, *who* stacks stones, strolls to Steve's Sweet Shoppe.
                            or
    Stanley, *who* strolls to Steve's Sweet Shoppe, stacks stones.
2. Melissa and Martina, *who* model muumuus at Marshall's, also marketed moccasins in Monterey.
3. James Harrington Chadwick, *who* is the chauffeur for Brigadier General Horace Honor, speaks Swahili.
4. Mt. Saint Helens, *which* erupted on May 18th, destroyed thousands of acres of forest.
5. My mother, *whose* polka-dotted coat hung in the closet, worked for a toy company.
6. You and Delbert, *whose* good luck it is to be in the Paul Robeson High School attendance area, are graduating eighth-graders.
7. You, *who* led everyone else in sales this month, are the newest salesman in the company.
8. I was given the unclaimed fly swatter, *which* I turned into the office.
9. The troopers, *whose* horses couldn't be ridden much farther, struggled in the deep snow.
10. Our rent, *which* is due today, will cause our eviction if we don't pay it.

COMBINING WITH ING WORDS, page 54

EXERCISE 3, page 55   POSSIBLE ANSWERS

1. Lynne, *driving* a sports car, easily out-drags everybody else.
                            or
    Lynne, easily *out-dragging* everybody else, drives a sports car.
2. *Looking* for the boy, Sheila found him in the trash can.
3. *Noticing* that many of the little ones are missing, Carolyn feeds her guppies.
4. We smiled nervously at Count Dracula, *wishing* we had not gone to his castle.
5. Whitney, *wearing* her Batgirl costume, jumped from the top of the jungle gym.
6. The baby, *smiling* happily, smeared glue in her hair.

7. The parakeet, *whistling* "Dixie" in its cage, amuses Orville.
8. *Beating* the heat, the pig snorts contentedly in the mud.
9. Beth opens the surprise package, *finding* it contains only a rabbit's-foot key chain.
10. *Teaching* spiders to make lace, Mr. Tattan has become rich.

COMMA RULE 4, page 55

Again, be sure students have time to adequately discuss this rule after they have just seen its **FUNCTION** in use. If you're using a punctuation chart in front of the classroom, you can add all new rules as a visual referent.

EXERCISE 4, page 56   POSSIBLE ANSWERS

Flip Flop--Either sentence may become the ING phrase.

1. *Throwing* her hands into the air, the goalie blocked the shot.
                              or
   Blocking the shot, the goalie threw her hands into the air.
2. *Smashing* the serve out of her opponent's reach, Aggie won the match point.
3. *Departing* with a tear in her eye, Grace kissed her mother good-bye.
4. *Escaping* from his brothers, Matthew Thomas ran at full speed.
5. *Racing* toward home plate, Lou attempted to break the tie game.

COMBINING AND CREATING A PARAGRAPH REVIEW, page 57

EXERCISE 5, The Mouse House, page 57   HERE IS ONE POSSIBLE COMBINATION.

1. There is a small hole in the kitchen wall. **2.** Carrying cheese in its mouth, a tiny, brown mouse runs out of the hole. **3.** Suddenly, the mouse panics as it sees a cat which is about to pounce on it. **4.** The mouse enters the hole, feeling happy and safe. **5.** Feeling sorry for itself, the hungry cat moans.

You may need to help get students started with this exercise. If so, combine sentences 1, 2, and 3 as a class and then gradually ease students into the rest as an independent exercise. Be sure to orally share some finished products.

Even the Best Don't Win Every Time

Here is one possible story. The words used for connection are underlined.

Frosty Gill, <u>who</u> was a brain surgeon, was muscular and lean. <u>Standing</u> over 6'6" barefoot, he was an impressive looking man. <u>Although</u> he was an All-American basketball player, he had studied medicine <u>because</u> he wished to help the sick. <u>Since</u> he was outstanding, he was offered several professional contracts. However, he became a brain surgeon <u>because</u> he was a helpful person. <u>Whenever</u> Frosty performed surgery, he worked with great care <u>and</u> prayerful concern for his patients.

He knew he would have to perform a miracle <u>when</u> the emergency room called him <u>on</u> Monday night. <u>While</u> <u>walking</u> her dog, a little girl had been struck <u>by</u> a hit-and-run driver <u>whose</u> car had no headlights.

The tiny patient, <u>who</u> was unconscious <u>on</u> the operating table, had only a slim chance <u>of</u> <u>surviving</u> her head injuries. Dr. Gill worked tirelessly <u>over</u> the child all night <u>fighting</u> to save her life. In spite of his heroic efforts, the little girl died without regaining consciousness. <u>As</u> Dr. Frosty Gill walked <u>out</u> <u>of</u> the hospital <u>in</u> the wet, grey dawn, he wished there was overtime <u>in</u> this life-and-death game.

Review **The Stack the Deck Writing Process** on pages 4-9 in this guide before teaching this assignment.

STAGE ONE: PREWRITING, page 62

STUDENT OBJECTIVES AND EVALUATION SHEET

The grading sheet or SOES appears on **page 63** in this guide. You can introduce it any time although before the **DRAFTING** stage is your best bet.

By now you should be familiar with all facets of a process which includes helpful drills, prewriting, first draft, **SOS**, proofreading, and rewriting.

The mode shifts one last time--this time to fast paced action, using **ING words**. Each **HELPFUL DRILL** is intended to lead up to writing the first draft.

HELPFUL DRILL 1--ING WORDS TO THE RESCUE, page 62
POSSIBLE ANSWERS

1. The flag was waving in the wind.
2. Yan Ken was jumping over the hedges.
3. Dashing through the mud, Willie crossed the goal line.
4. The ducks were flying south for the winter.
5. Listening to the music made Lorenzo happy.
6. Milking a cow, Old man MacDonald was kicked in the ribs.
7. Shirley is singing in the shower.
8. The blowing wind tore the awnings from the building.
9. The frightened child, screaming in terror, ran from the haunted house.
10. Fixing a bike tire can be tiresome.

HELPFUL DRILL 2--ING WORDS AS ADJECTIVES, page 62

There is an infinite set of answers for this exercise. Why not use a transparency and have your students complete this activity orally?

HELPFUL DRILL 3--SHOWING ACTION THROUGH VERBS, page 63
POSSIBLE ANSWERS

1. The old-fashioned radiator leaked, flooding the basement.
2. Driving through the alley, the policewoman noticed an open window.
3. Racing through the hallway, Nick tripped over the pencil.
4. Sizzling on the grill, the hamburger looked mouth-watering.
5. The eagle, soaring high in the heavens, peered down on the tiny mouse.
6. Rumbling down the highway, the tractors caused a traffic jam.
7. Quietly tiptoeing into my room, the tooth fairy left a dollar under my pillow.
8. Sammy, arriving early for the surprise party, helped Carmen decorate the basement.

THINK SHEET, pages 65-66

Be sure to have students use their own paper for this **Think Sheet**. Again, modeling can really help. Ask students to complete **NUMBER 1** on their own **Think Sheets** and share some samples with the entire class. This should allow you to trouble shoot to be sure that students are including enough specific details.

STAGE TWO: WRITING THE FIRST DRAFT, page 67

SENTENCE OPENING SHEET, page 67

The student sample paper on page 59 can also be used as a paper to practice the **Sentence Opening Sheet**. If you feel your students need this practice, have them complete an **SOS** for this paper and then have them review each of the 5 points together. If you sense that your students have mastered this process, then have them proceed directly on to completing their own **Sentence Opening Sheets**.

STAGE THREE: REWRITING, page 68

STUDENT MODEL--The Answer to a Maiden's Prayer, page 59

Discuss the analysis of the student model with the entire class. When students move to using the **Checklist** for their own papers, you may wish to have them read the narratives aloud to each other first and then answer question number 6 as a beginning.

STAGE FOUR: PUBLISHING, page 70

As another publishing suggestion, here's one you might consider. Choose four or five of the best papers and have cooperative groups draw a cartoon strip to match one of the narratives of their choice. Various responsibilities might include:

> a) developing the story board--all group members;
> b) preparing initial illustrations--one or two students;
> c) adding dialogue boxes--one or two students; or
> d) adding color and headings--one or two students.

The resulting strips plus the narrative would be great to publish in a collective book for parents or for an OPEN HOUSE display. If at all possible, having a real cartoonist come to describe his/her work process would be ideal. You might consider sprinkling any students with artistic abilities around evenly to various groups.

CONNECTING AND PERSUADING

STUDENT LEARNING OBJECTIVES

1. The student will discuss never-heard-before verbs.
2. The student will create his own never heard before verbs.
3. The student will combine sentences with verbs.
4. The student will combine sentences using the connectors--**and, but, or**.
5. The student will punctuate compound sentences correctly.
6. The student will write a business letter following a standard format.

ORAL LANGUAGE INTO WRITING

NEVER HEARD BEFORE VERBS, page 71

WARM-UP ACTIVITY 1, page 71

This is a fun activity. Read the sentences aloud and have your students figure out the meanings.

Here are two examples.

9. **Bucketed** means to shoot a basketball through the hoop.
15. **Grandslammed** means to hit a home run in baseball with the bases full.

ADDING VERBS TO OUR LANGUAGE, page 72

WARM-ACTIVITY 2, page 72

This would make an excellent cooperative learning activity. In groups, students could write their own sentences. While some groups are writing on paper, others could write on overhead projector transparencies to be used for a group discussion. In fact, instead of students working individually on **WARM-UP ACTIVITY 3**, you might have them compose a group paragraph for some of their favorite creative sentences.

12. Brand new meaning: "Michael Jordan **skied** from the free throw line."

   (Former Basketball star Michael Jordan jumps so high into the air that he just about floats in the sky--*skied*.)

SENTENCE MANIPULATION

COMBINING SENTENCES WITH VERBS, page 73

EXERCISE 1, pages 73-74

1. Minnie made mud pies, baked them carefully, and gobbled them down.
2. The actress painted her wrinkled skin, glued on false eyelashes, and plopped on a bright red wig.
3. The puppet came to life, danced with the teddy bears, and then went back to sleep.
4. The pinch hitter bounced a single to center, slid into second base, and swallowed a pound of dust.
5. We made our beds, hung up our clothes, and hated every minute of it.

COMBINING WITH *AND, BUT,* AND *OR,* page 74

Note: Some students may need more explanation in understanding the role **and, but,** and **or** play in a sentence. To aid in clarifying, perhaps this will help.

> **and** is used when you want the reader to continue in the same direction
> **but** indicates a change, exception or contrast
> **or** offers a choice

EXERCISE 2, page 74   POSSIBLE ANSWERS

1. My little brother, Davey, made my bed for me, **and** I wondered if he had short-sheeted* it.
2. I wanted to paint my room red and black, **but** my mom looked sick and said, "No!"
3. Hector could walk to the movie, **or** he could sit at home and sulk.
4. Professor Sagorsky had picked the Lotto Jackpot numbers, **and/but** he threw away the winning ticket by mistake.
5. With my graduation gift I can buy a CD player, **or** I can donate the money to the homeless.
* **Note**: Contemporary students may not be familiar with the prank of *short-sheeting*.

COMMA RULE # 5, page 75

Review Comma Rule 1. Make sure your students have written the rule in their punctuation rules notebook as is suggested at the end of Unit 1.

EXERCISE 3, page 75   POSSIBLE ANSWERS

1. Arief must cut the lawn, or he will not receive his allowance.
2. I tried to change Sly Sylvester's mind, but it was a hopeless attempt.
3. The fleas in my bedroom are big and hungry, and they don't make my bed either.
4. The tractor rolled over the muddy ground, and/but the cows looked unconcerned as the contraption approached.
5. My homework isn't finished, and/but my favorite program starts in five minutes.

To reinforce the Comma Rule, you may want to offer a bonus point for each correctly punctuated answer.

> **NOTE:** Stress the use of the comma **before** the glue word. Point out that the *glue word/comma* combination is **only** used when joining **two complete sentences**. Students will probably need to be reminded of this rule in future work, as it is easily overlooked. In a sentence with only a compound predicate, there is no comma used. Model both examples. See below.

Example 1:   Compound Sentence

    I went to the game, and I bought a souvenir sweatshirt.

Example 2:   Compound Predicate

    I went to the game and bought a souvenir sweatshirt.

USING YOUR WRITER'S VOCABULARY TO COMPOSE, page 76

EXERCISE 4--Swamp Madness, page 76

Have the students combine the sentence pairs (one pair at a time) and then go back and write a paragraph using each new sentence. This will be less confusing for students.

    Here is a possible answer:

> The night was evil, **and** the man in the moon had an innocent smile
>
> on his face. Gentle waves lapped at the rocks, **and** the water lilies decorated
>
> the shadows of the lake. The lovely lake seemed peaceful enough, **but**
>
> beneath the murky waters lurked the creature. Tonight it was hungry **and**
>
> was searching the shoreline for food. The victim must be found before
>
> daybreak, **or** the creature will go hungry.

EXTENSION ACTIVITY: Have your students create an exciting ending for this exercise, reminding them of appropriate vs. inappropriate school writing.

CONNECTING THE SKILLS, page 76

EXERCISE 5, pages 76-77

Because of the latitude involved in this exercise, students may find it a little more difficult. You may want to get students started by working on the board or overhead. Or you may think it necessary to use the entire exercise as a **class project**, then allow students to write individual endings. You be the judge of your students' comfort level. Whatever the case, individual stories should be shared orally in class.

> Review **The Stack the Deck Writing Process** on pages 4-9 in this guide before teaching this assignment.

STAGE ONE: PREWRITING, page 78

STUDENT OBJECTIVE AND EVALUATION SHEET--SCORING RUBRIC

Open the Deck provides students with opportunities to write in various modes. This unit's mode is **persuasive**, which is more demanding for many young writers because it requires making a reasoned argument. To insure student success, this persuasive topic is structured with examples, suggestions, and steps to follow.

Distribute copies of the **Student Objectives and Evaluation Sheet (SOES)** from **page 64** in this guide.

Be sure your class understands the different purposes for friendly letters and business letters on page 78. Also, discuss *tone*. How does the letter sound to the reader (polite or pushy, calm or angry, confident or shaky, serious or joking).

FOCUSED WRITING TRAIT, PAGE 79

Be certain your students understand what the two traits mean; they are this unit's targets.

BUSINESS LETTER FORMAT, page 80

Either basic style is acceptable. If you have a preference, however, tell your class. Remind them that in the **heading** and **inside address** the city, state, and zip code go together on the second line.

EXERCISE 6, page 81

The **greeting** now includes the option of non-gender-bias, such as *Dear Sir or Madam:* or *Dear Sir or Ms.:* .

EXERCISE 7, page 81

All examples end with a colon (:). Check to see if any students used the non-gender-bias greeting in **EXERCISE 6**.

EVALUATING BUSINESS LETTERS, page 82

Ask the class to evaluate both versions of Wayne's letter on page 82 using the five key parts listed on page 82.

WRITING PROMPT, page 84

Students have a choice between a letter of complaint for a product or a service. If you have internet access, try the US Government's Consumer Product Safety Commission(CSPC) web site at *www.cpsc.gov>* and click "recall news." Or visit Consumer Reports magazine's recall page at *www. consumerreports. org/recalls/index /html>*

BUSINESS LETTER THINK SHEET, pages 85-86

Question 1 could be from a catalog. Question 6 could have several tones, like polite and firm. Question 8 could be skipped if the complaint is for a service. Question 12: point out the 2 *e's* in *Sincerely*' have interested students sign-up in advance, so you can control the flow.

STAGE TWO: WRITING THE FIRST DRAFT, page 87

Remember that the flow of ideas is key, not perfection. Also, decide beforehand how to handle students' desire to share their drafts-in-progress with other students. Enthusiasm and sharing are important, but so is a quiet writing environment. One suggestion is to create a *Sharing Corner* somewhere for two students at a time who are eager to share what they are writing; have interested students sign up in advance so you can control the flow.

STAGE THREE: REWRITING, page 87

To encourage helpful, thoughtful feedback from peers, consider modeling the use of the **Checklist** on page 88. Put a sample letter(remove student's name) on an overhead transparency, and show the class how to fill out the **Checklist** questions. This modeling uses the *Think Aloud* strategy of revealing to students what you are thinking as you evaluate a letter. Also, awarding points or a grade to student checklist answers increases student helpfulness.

STAGE FOUR: PUBLISHING, page 90

For students who wrote a fictitious business letter, consider mailing them to a consumer rights organization for feedback. Your school or public library will have names and addresses of such organizations. Perhaps one would agree to read the letters and respond to the students.

STUDENT LEARNING OBJECTIVES

1. The student will discuss multiple meanings of the same word.
2. The student will discuss the meanings of idioms.
3. The student will write Tom Swifties.
4. The student will identify sentence fragments which are signaled by **glue**, **WH**, and **ING words**.
5. The student will read sentences in a paragraph in reverse order to *hear* sentence fragments.
6. The student will correct sentence fragments.
7. The student will write a narrative about a personal memory.
8. The student will write in first person point of view.
9. The student will keep all the verbs in the past tense.

ORAL LANGUAGE INTO WRITING

MANY MEANINGS OF A WORD, page 91

WARM--UP ACTIVITY 1, page 91   **POSSIBLE ANSWERS**

As an introduction to this unit it might be fun to see what the students think these words mean orally **before** the they even open their books. After a discussion of the different meanings (cited from the boys' and girls' examples), the students may open their books and then do Activity 1. (Some students will feel more confident doing it this way.)

WARM-UP ACTIVITY 2, page 92   **POSSIBLE ANSWERS**

1. <u>Cup</u> your hand, so I can put this <u>cup</u> there.
2. The bread was so stale that the <u>duck</u> had to <u>duck</u> when I threw it.
3. When Jonah goes camping, he takes a <u>light</u> <u>light</u> with him.
4. I knew the <u>soil</u> in the garden would <u>soil</u> my pants.
5. To have to <u>bore</u> these holes in the wood all day is a <u>bore</u>!

STRETCHED MEANINGS--IDIOMS, page 92

WARM-UP ACTIVITY 4, page 93

1. Give me a *hand*.
2. Shake my *hand*.
3. The audience gave the performer a *hand*.
4. the minute *hand* of a clock
5. Drawing the ace gave me the winning *hand*.
6. the ranch's hired *hand*
7. first *hand* knowledge
8. in good *hands* with Allstate
9. She had a *hand* in the decision.
10. The party got out of *hand*.

An alternative approach to teaching sentence fragments as *incomplete ideas* is presented in this unit. Instead of merely instructing students to look for *missing subject, verb, or complete thoughts*, students will be taught how to identify and to correct fragments using sentence combining techniques. Fragments will be described as *lonesome parts of combined kernel sentences.*

Since many fragments begin with **glue, WH,** and **ING words,** students will be instructed: 1) to be on alert for fragments when these combining words begin sentences, and 2) to recognize the missing part of fragments. For example, *Walking without her camel* is a fragment: it is lonesome for a part, and it begins with an **ING word.** Students will learn to be on alert when an **ING word** phrase stands by itself, and they will be taught to find the missing part: *I saw Irza walking without her camel* or *Walking without her camel, Irza carried the snow shovels.*

FRAGMENT TIP NUMBER 1, page 94

EXERCISE 1, page 94   **(Glue Words, WH Words, ING Words)**

Students may refer back to pages 40 and 64 for glue word and WH word collections to help spot them in the sentences, **or** they should look at the handy-dandy wall charts you made.

1.	starting	6.	until
2.	which	7.	while
3.	in order to	8.	until
4.	because	9.	waiting
5.	leaving	10.	even though

FRAGMENT TIP NUMBER 2, page 95

EXERCISE 2, page 95 **(Frag or OK)**

1.	frag	6.	OK
2.	frag	7.	frag
3.	OK	8.	frag
4.	frag	9.	OK
5.	frag	10.	frag

EXERCISE 3, page 96 **(Frag or OK)**

1.	frag	6.	frag
2.	OK	7.	OK
3.	frag	8.	OK
4.	frag	9.	frag
5.	OK	10.	frag

DIFFICULT TO SPOT FRAGMENTS, page 97

EXERCISE 4 --Harold the Hot Dog, page 98

1. frag
2. frag
3. OK
4. frag
5. frag
6. frag
7. frag
8. OK
9. frag
10. OK
11. frag
12. frag
13. frag
14. OK
15. frag

EXERCISE 5 --(DOER/DID), page 98

1. DOER
*2. DOER
3. DOER
4. DOER
5. DID
6. DOER
7. DOER
8. DID

*The DOER is incomplete. Since this is a Pred. Nom. case, you may have to do some extra explaining.

CORRECTING FRAGMENTS, page 99

EXERCISE 6, pages 100-101   POSSIBLE ANSWERS

1. Forgetful Foster parks his juicy wad of chewing gum beneath my math book.
2. Steady Eddie Stanwick, the star state trooper, speeds to the scene of the accident, leaving his ticket book back at Pancho's Diner.
3. A silver-tipped hawk glided down to Randy, who had raised it from birth.
4. Winston wagged his tail when Cornflakes landed on his head.
5. A few elderly elephants have rolled over onto my side of the bed.
6. "Oh, no!" cried Roberto in shock, watching his pet guinea pig ride off on his pogo stick.
7. Smiling, yellow daisies are growing tall beside the railroad tracks outside of town.
8. Several space travelers landed in Ms. Hooper's flower garden even though they were aiming for the swimming pool.
9. Maisie moistens Mom's famous pie dough which is the secret step in the recipe.
10. Jane earns extra money training bumble bees to play slide trombones.

EXERCISE 7, page 101   FRAGMENTS EXPANDED INTO SENTENCES

1. The prestidigitator who juggles golf balls accidentally swallowed one.
2. A big, fat possum lazily snoozes on our roof.
3. Handsome Harold with big, blue eyes strolled around the sunny swimming pool.
4. The high-diving tower with fifty-nine steps reflected off Harold's sunglasses, drawing his attention.
5. Miserable Max bricked up the door to his bedroom so that no one could enter.

EXERCISE 8, page 101-102

The answers will vary. Why not complete this as a cooperative learning activity?

Review **The Stack the Deck Writing Process** on pages 4-9 in this guide before teaching this assignment.

STAGE ONE: PREWRITING, page 103

STUDENT OBJECTIVES AND EVALUATION SHEET-SCORING RUBRIC

The **SOES** sheet for this assignment is on **page 65** in this guide.

WHERE DO I START?, page 103

If some students need to review regular and irregular verbs, work with them before starting these drills. Then, these drills will encourage them as they reinforce what you taught them.

Helpful Drill 1: Examining a Past Tense Paper, pages 104

When all students have finished the analysis sheet:

1. Be sure that the subject-verb chart is covered with the entire class. This is necessary for a good start to the unit. It's probably a good idea to cover the entire analysis sheet, using feedback from different students.

2. Numbers 6-7 should serve as a reminder that the model exhibits some good sentence variety. Try to keep reinforcing skills covered in past chapters.

Helpful Drill 2: Practicing as a Group, page 106

(**NOTE:** You may want to introduce this practice the day before you do it. This will allow students a chance to think about possible topics overnight.)

1. When students finish their planning lists, ask different students to volunteer to share theirs with the class.

2. It would be a good idea for the teacher to make a list, too. This can be put on the board or an overhead, and it will serve as a good model. It also shows the teacher in a composing role, which is important for students to see.

WRITING PROMPT - SUBJECT OF YOUR MEMORY, page 108

As a prewriting activity, share some frightening, embarrassing, joyous, or sad moments in your life. These personal stories might serve as a catalyst for your students to share their own memories.

THINK SHEET, page 109

Be sure to check student **Think Sheets** to see if individuals are on the right track. Again, the teacher could complete a **Think Sheet** for one of her personal memories. However, this should be shared only after students have filled out their own **Think Sheets**. Otherwise there is too great a temptation to closely *model* the teacher.

Remind the students to use all their senses when they start thinking about what to write--what they saw, heard, felt, smelled, hoped, feared, realized, noticed, thought, and so on.

In addition, it may be a good idea to check each student's number 6 on the Think Sheet. Check to see if the beginning and end verify that it is limited in time and space. This can be modeled as a class activity with students orally sharing or can be a perfect way to conference with each student individually.

STAGE TWO: WRITING THE FIRST DRAFT, page 110

THE SENTENCE OPENING SHEET, pages 110-111

The use of the complete **Sentence Opening Sheet** is explained thoroughly. Remember, however, to focus on just one column at a time until students have covered the information for that column thoroughly.

The teacher should carefully monitor and guide the use of the **SOS** sheet in a step by step instructional manner. Go slowly, explain carefully! The **Sentence Opening Sheet** appears on page 42 in the student text.

STAGE THREE: REWRITING, page 112

CHECKLIST SHEET, pages 112-113

It may be helpful for the teacher to select proofreading partners. This way it's easier o pair a student with someone appropriate. For example, friends are sometimes reluctant to carefully and constructively criticize each others' papers.

It is important for the teacher to establish a serious tone about proofreading. Stress its importance and the need for good proofreading in order to produce a good finished product.

Provide your students with an opportunity to share their Memory Papers with the class. Some possible options: students can read their papers to the whole class or to smaller groups. They can illustrate their memory paper and display it in the classroom, hallway, a prominent place, or they can make a *Class Memory Book* with all papers included as an anthology.

STAGE FOUR: PUBLISHING, page 114

As an alternate publishing activity, you might have students give speeches of their personal moments.

STUDENT LEARNING OBJECTIVES

1. The student will write *Sniglets*.
2. The student will identify run-on sentences by reading sentences aloud to *hear* the error.
3. The student will correct run-ons by adding WH, glue, and ING Words.
4. The student will correct run-ons by using Connector Words (coordinating conjunctions).
5. The student will correct run-ons by separating ideas into two sentences.
6. The student will write a short paper which describes an event as if it were *unfolding* before your eyes.
7. The student will correctly and consistently use the present tense verb in his or her paper.
8. The student will follow consistent organizing and editing procedures in writing his or her paper.

ORAL LANGUAGE INTO WRITING

CREATING NEW WORDS, page 115

WARM-UP ACTIVITY 1, page 116

1. a notebook that breaks open onto the floor	d. **bindbreaker**
2. a pencil with no eraser on top	b. **balder**
3. sound a skateboard makes when the wheels are turned sharply	a. **scrooch**
4. a piece of Scotch tape peeled off to be used again	e. **Botch tape**
5. a burned out lightbulb	c. **blub**

WARM-UP ACTIVITY 2, pages 116-117

This is an excellent cooperative learning activity. Have a contest to see which group can create the most original names. Send any great ones to us. We love to collect student samples.

Make up a poster of all the new words created by your students. It might not only be fun but an eye-opening experience to see how many coined words the students come up with.

RUN-ON SENTENCES, page 118

Run-on sentences are probably the most common error in the writing of young students (all students?!). Instead of attempting to teach students that run-ons are *two sentences that run together*, this unit will present run-ons as two combined kernels with missing **glue**, **WH**, and **ING words**.

Students will be taught to identify the two kernels in a run-on sentence and to supply the needed connection to remove their error. This approach is consistent with the skills acquired from the previous units. In addition, the more common methods of correcting run-ons, using conjunctions and separating ideas, will be practiced.

EXERCISE 1, page 118   **Complete this as an oral activity.**

1. Mom and Dad groaned / the repair bill for the dryer was $130.
2. Jeb dashed behind the barrel / Janet scrambled up a tree.
3. A black spider smiles to itself / a careless fly zooms toward his web.
4. Mr. Birosak from Tunaville packed his suitcase / he forgot his train ticket on the dresser.
5. Roger raced sixteen blocks home / he was late for dinner.
6. A young duck floated in the moat / the crocodiles played water polo.
7. Billy Walters blew his harmonica / the band blasted music behind him.
8. A pair of eggs sizzled in the frying pan / the smell reached the camper's nose.
9. The bucket leaks / water drips out.
10. Frances arrowed her bow / the wolf stood frozen in the night.

EXERCISE 2, pages 118-119

1. ...whiskers / the...
2. ...tacos / he...
3. ...toenails/ she...
4. ...bread / it...
5. ...desk / her...
6. ...repair / it...
7. ...first / the...
8. ...lunch / a...
9. ...karate / she...
10. ...river / each...

EXERCISE 3 --He Needed a Vacation, page 119

1. in...badly   (a)
2. he...office   (a)
3. buying...Oregon   (b)
4. there...friends   (c)
5. each...late   (d)
6. they...days   (d)
7. early...jogging   (e)
8. tired...bed   (f)
9. after...jogging   (f)
10. he...sweat   (g)
11. the...them   (h)
12. huffing...up   (i)
13. he...though   (i)
14. the...again   (j)
15. by...it   (j)
16. his...day   (k)
17. he...better   (l)
18. he...Marathon   (l)
19. his...Frank   (m)
20. little...flying   (m)

Note: Sentence 11 could end with *huffing and puffing*.

CORRECTING RUN-ONS WITH ING, WH, AND GLUE WORDS, page 120

EXERCISE 4, pages 120-121 The glue word choices for **c** in each set are flexible.

Remind students that objects, animals, and ideas use "that" as a WH word.

1. a. picking
   b. who
   c. while
2. a. watching
   b. who
   c. as
3. a. charging
   b. that
   c. after

4. a. using
   b. who
   c. When
5. a. cutting
   b. that
   c. When

EXERCISE 5, page 121   **POSSIBLE ANSWERS**

1. Dolores naps in the bay window dreaming of sardine sandwiches.
2. As the king's castle appeared before us, dark clouds covered the pointy towers of the battlements.
3. Paddling breathlessly across the pond, Oswald the Otter spotted a fox on the bank.
4. Our friend, who did magic tricks, vanished her younger brother, Robbie.
5. When Rhonda Rockette set the school record, she ran the 60-yard dash in 9.5 seconds.
6. After a few crumbs tumbled from the picnic table, a scouting party of ants noticed.
7. Since the dishwasher is broken, I now wash the supper dishes by hand.
8. Herman the Vermin, creeping through the cellar, avoids mousetraps.
9. Before a gold streak of sunlight peeked through the clouds, raindrops stopped falling.
10. After Rolando finished his violin lesson, he hurried outside to his bike.

CORRECTING RUN-ONS WITH *BOYS FAN* WORDS, page 122

EXERCISE 6   (Underline Connector Word--Conjunction), page 122

1. ..., so...
2. ..., but...
3. ..., and...

4. ..., yet...
5. ..., or...

EXERCISE 7 (Connector Words), page 122 Urge students to use at least five different Connector Words.

1. ...fry, so, but...
2. ...horn, for...
3. ...night, and...

4. ...Motel, or...
5. ...garden, but...
6. ...order, for...

Because students have no trouble using (over-using) the connector word **and**, encourage them to learn the use of the other six connector words. In fact, you can enforce flexibility by limiting the use of **and** in their written work. Likewise, the misuse of stringing kernels together with **and** . . . **but** . . . **so** . . . can be stopped by permitting only two connector words per sentence.

EXERCISE 8, page 123   **Correct Run-on Sentences**

This exercise really hits home when the students read the numbered sets **aloud**.

1 a.	Fourteen...ramp	4 a.	Carefully...cages
1 b.	at...runway.	4 b.	even...part
2 a.	The...cages	5 a.	Settling...eyes
2 b.	Debra's...lions.	5 b.	with...bike.
3 a.	The...weight		
3 b.	all...black		

FRAGMENT AND RUN-ON FINALE, page 124

Exercise 9--Man's Best Friend, page 124

1.	frag	6.	frag	13.	OK	2.	OK
3.	frag	9.	frag	14.	frag	7.	OK
4.	RO	10.	frag	15.	OK	8.	OK
5.	RO	12	frag			11.	OK

Review **The Stack the Deck Writing Process** on pages 4-9 in this guide before teaching this assignment.

STAGE ONE: PREWRITING, page 126

STUDENT OBJECTIVES AND EVALUATION SHEET-SCORING RUBRIC

See **page 66** in this guide for a model grading sheet for this assignment.

Special Teaching Tip

Linda Goss, the English Department Chairperson at Alf J. Mapp Junior High School in Portsmouth, Virginia, offered the following suggestion as a prewriting strategy for use with the observation paper.

"Prior to presenting the lesson on the observation paper, I planned an intruder episode with another English teacher. While I was discussing the observation paper with my students, the other teacher would burst into my room and confront me about some problem she was having with the work I had given her. Needless to say, she was to appear distraught and angry over the situation. On the day of this incident, following the intruder act, my students were floored by this teacher's action and some of the students even volunteered to *get her* when she ran out of the room, slamming the door. After the students calmed down, I explained our act and instructed them to write about what they had just observed. We then shared the observations and were ready to begin an observation of their own.

"This prewriting strategy proved very helpful in setting the stage, and it gave the students a better sense of how to convey the action in their own writing."

A NOTE OF CAUTION: Because of the current tension in US schools, this activity should only be used in a controlled setting with the right circumstances and the right student population.

Students must understand the necessary detachment of this paper: they are distant observers, not active participants. Therefore, no use of **I** or **me**. **Note**: In sentence 7 of **The Terrified Skier** student model on page 125, the present tense verb is *is*.

Show your class the following pairs of verbs:

is--was
am--was
are--were
has--had

HELPFUL DRILLS, page 126

EXERCISE 13, page 129

1.	past	4.	past
2.	past	5.	present
3.	present	6.	present

The Terrified Skier Analysis Sheet, page 130

Again, be sure to cover the Analysis Sheet exercise with the entire class when students have finished their own. Provide extra help to those students who seem to be having difficulty.

WRITING PROMPT, page 131

Brainstorm for more possible topics and/or meaningful observations: Idea starters: *Something I'll never forget that I saw . . .   Funniest thing I saw . . .*

YOUR ATTENTION PLEASE, page 131

Practice examples of this form orally with the students in order to let them get the hang of it. You may need to model one or two at the chalkboard or on the overhead to help build confidence with this writing technique.

ORGANIZING YOUR IDEAS, page 132

The tense flow of this paper may be a bit more difficult for students to *hear* with their inner ear. For that reason, the **class project** described on page 132 is particularly important. Spend as much time needed here as necessary. Students will have difficulty with their own **Think Sheets** unless they have a good feel for the pattern which has been established with the entire class.

OBSERVATION PAPER THINK SHEET, page 133

Be sure to pay special attention to number 6 on the **Think Sheet**. If students are having trouble getting started, sit down with them and get the ball rolling. This information will be vital for writing a complete paper later on.

Check off satisfactory completion of the **Think Sheet**.

STAGE TWO: WRITING THE FIRST DRAFT, page 134

Just a thought on number 8--Try to add a new word you invented for this paper. This relates to *creating new words* earlier in this unit.

SENTENCE OPENING SHEET, pages 134-135

As before, be sure that you have your students follow the explicit directions in the text for each column on the **SOS**. This time the **SOS** has 4 columns.

STAGE THREE: REWRITING, page 136

As in the previous unit, a sample paper entitled " Big Trouble" is provided to help students learn to spot potential problems.

OBSERVATION PAPER CHECKLIST, page 137

STAGE FOUR: PUBLISHING, page 138

Again, encourage public sharing of this paper. Students can role-play TV announcers or newspaper reporters by reading their final copies to the class. Or better yet, set up a tape recorder or video camera for them to use.

STUDENT LEARNING OBJECTIVES

1. The student will explain the meaning of flip-flopped words.
2. The student will rearrange a sentence, preserving the same meaning in the new sentence she writes.
3. The student will add variety to her sentence openings.
4. The student will compose a writing across the curriculum composition.

ORAL LANGUAGE INTO WRITING

FLEXIBLE WORDS, page 139

As always, we begin a unit with an oral activity. Have the students play with the language to see how some English words function as both verbs and nouns (objects).

WARM-UP ACTIVITY 1, pages 139-140

1.	Rodney paints bags.	serves as a painter decorating shopping bags.
2.	Rodney dresses cuts.	works as a medic.
3.	Rodney walks shovels.	works as a clerk in a hardware store, helping customers carry out shovels.
4.	Rodney fences guards.	breaks out of prison using a sword.
5.	Rodney trails marks.	is a hunter on patrol for deer or is a detective investigating a crime
6.	Rodney soaps boxes.	is in the shipping department of a company, using recycled containers that need cleaning

(One 6th grader described the original job *Rodney boxes soaps* as *placing video cassettes of soap operas into boxes to ship to TV stations.*)

7.	Rodney drawers locks.	works as a locksmith. He's called to install locks on desk drawers.
8.	Rodney covers snaps.	is in the notions department of a fabric store.

WARM-UP ACTIVITY 2--The Big Blizzard, page 140

This can be a challenging activity. Consider having the students work on this in their cooperative learning groups in order to help each other out and share ideas. You may even suggest to them that this will be a contest to see which group comes up with the most original and creative paragraph.

EXTENSION ACTIVITY: See if the class can find more words that function as both nouns and verbs in order to create more flip-flopped jobs for Rodney. A dictionary search for (n.) and (v.) might help.

REARRANGING, page 141

Rearranging sentences serves to reinforce a student's belief in her power over language. The many options available for sentence variety also become more apparent. Verbal sharing of new sentences is always a good idea for students. You will notice that each exercise is just a little more demanding. This should make it easier for students to gradually build their skills.

EXERCISE 1, page 141   POSSIBLE ANSWERS

1. Jennifer flipped her strained spinach on the floor and yelled at the baby-sitter.
2. Last night, Clem Periwinkle ate creamed catfish for dinner.
3. Climbing into the sky, the multi-colored balloon lurched wildly.
4. Smiling at anybody and everybody all the time gave the beauty queen lock jaw.
5. The Slovak baker, Georgio, makes cream pies and hot cross buns as he sings.
6. Norman stubbed his toe when he jumped into the huge vat of Jell-O.
7. On a stormy night Little Lester walked into the haunted house cautiously.
8. Immediately stick an apple in the roasted pig's mouth when it is finished.
9. In the wood stove at home, Shawna made twenty dozen chocolate chip cookies.
10. Cheetah screamed angrily, "Get it yourself ape man!"

COMBINING AND REARRANGING, page 142

EXERCISE 2, page 142   POSSIBLE ANSWERS

1. The enormous spaceship, with the blinking lights, was receiving a speeding ticket.
   For speeding, the enormous spaceship with the blinking lights, was receiving a ticket.
2. Strolling through the waves, the green octopus played the accordion.
   The green octopus played the accordion as he strolled through the waves.
3. The carefully toasted marshmallow was melted onto the chocolate square.
   The marshmallow, which was carefully toasted, was melted onto the chocolate square.
4. The millionaire basketball player purchased the gold-painted car.
   The car, which was painted gold, was purchased by the millionaire basketball player.
5. In the morning, Seymour roller-skated four miles to school through the rain.
   Through the morning rain, Seymour roller-skated four miles to school.
6. Twice a day, the excited football players, who had new uniforms, practiced in the cold.
   The excited football players, who had new uniforms, practiced twice a day in the cold.
7. Swinging towards the smiling people, the cute monkey continued to search for fleas.
   The cute monkey swung towards the smiling people and searched for fleas.
8. The short, hot-dogging player slam-dunked the ball and let out a whoop.
   The hot-dogging player, who was short, let out a whoop when he/she slam-dunked the ball.

ANOTHER WRITER'S VOCABULARY PRACTICE, page 143

EXERCISE 3, pages 143-144

Answers will be as varied as those in **EXERCISE 2.**

Review **The Stack the Deck Writing Process** on pages 4-9 in this guide before teaching this assignment.

STAGE ONE: PREWRITING, page 145

In addition to becoming familiar with writing "traits," students also need to understand the various "modes" of writing they can use. This chapter introduces the expository mode. Be sure students understand this mode. You might want to consider bringing in some other examples of expository writing for sharing or for a bulletin board display.

STUDENT OBJECTIVES AND EVALUATION SHEET-SCORING RUBRIC

The grading sheet for this assignment appears on **page 67** in this guide.

WHERE DO I START? page 145

The intent of this writing assignment is to pull in a topic of study from some other academic discipline your students are experiencing. This could be science, social studies, health, the arts, even math.

Students begin by identifying **WHAT THEY KNOW**; then they use a few other sources to gather more information about **WHAT THEY WANT TO KNOW**. The intent here is not to make this a full-blown research report. That is addressed in much more detail in Unit 8. In fact, this assignment is a good prelude to the more demanding paper found at the end of the book.

It will be necessary for students to be able to locate a few other sources for additional information. You can work with your librarian or fellow teachers to help, but oral sources--even parents at home will suffice as a resource.

GETTING STARTED INVENTORY THINK SHEET, pages 147-151

It will be necessary to carefully review the **Think Sheet** format ahead of time. If you have the time, you might also consider developing a sample **Think Sheet** about a topic you know your students have recently studied.

Have students examine the complete Think Sheet sample in their book.

Also, here is a **second sample** of the **GETTING STARTED INVENTORY Think Sheet** which has been filled in by another student named Jennie Baker. You will notice that this student chose to investigate a topic she had been studying in science. Her choice was GENETICS IN SCIENCE AND BUSINESS.

GETTING STARTED INVENTORY THINK SHEET

NAME_____Jennie Baker_____Date_____Feb. 13_____

TOPIC OF INTEREST: ___Using Genetics in Business and Science_____

1. WHAT I KNOW:

a. Chromosomes in living cells carry the code of heredity.

b. Each chromosome is made of tiny parts called genes.

c. Dominant genes *rule over* some other genes because traits show up in a new organism.

d. Genes whose traits do not show up when paired with a dominant gene are called recessive genes.

e. Sudden changes in genes are called mutations.

2. WHAT I WANT TO KNOW:

a. Who studies mutations?

b. Can information about genes be used to help farmers?

c. My uncle, a farmer, said that genetics could mean big business and big bucks for ranchers. What did he mean?

d. What are some examples of mutations in animals or plants?

e. Why do mutations occur?

f. Who knows about this stuff in town?

3. WHERE I LOOKED:

Discovery magazine
Talked to Dr. Bob Sagor,
    our veterinarian
Talked to my uncle
Read my science text
Read two books suggested
    by the librarian

4. WHAT I DISCOVERED:

a. Scientists and agriculture specialists study genetic mutations.

b. Plant and animal breeders use genetics to improve animals and plants--and our food.

c. Researchers cross animal or plant parents to find out if the offspring have a trait.

d. By careful crossing, desirable genetic traits can be carried on to their offspring.

e. Some mutations in animals or plants become highly prized to farmers and ranchers.

f. Some examples of these valuable mutations are short legged sheep, hornless or "polled" cattle, thick skinned cattle and wilt resistant tomatoes.

g. Animals with the same mutations can be bred together to begin herds of animals with the same new traits.

h. Polled Herefords, Santa Gertrudis cattle and beefalo are all prized cattle who were developed through the study of genetics.

SELECTING A TOPIC, page 148

Be sure you conference with each student for three minutes or so as you help them select a topic from their brainstormed lists. If a topic is too broad or too esoteric, you can help redirect students towards a more manageable focus.

Also, you might want to post a notice in your faculty lounge a few weeks before this assignment begins informing your colleagues of the nature of this unit. You might be able to receive some suggested topics. In fact, you might make this project a joint venture. The assignment comes from another academic class; you teach the procedure in language arts.

HELPFUL DRILL 1--SUPPORTING STATEMENTS, page 152

This exercise could nicely lend itself to being completed in cooperative groups. As students search the sample **Think Sheet** to dig up supporting sentences, this might even be the most preferable mode as it helps students learn from each other.

HELPFUL DRILL 2--CATCHY OPENING, page 153

These **OPENING** examples require some fairly sophisticated analysis. Therefore, you'll want to guide students directly through the process. Again, a cooperative learning team approach could work well if you have set up the task well.

Students may come up with their own valid comments during this exercise. However, here are the most probable answers to the questions in the text.

Ideas for Your Discussion Questions, page 153

1. *EXAMPLE B* represents the best opening for the paper. It concisely identifies the topic to be described, and it teases the reader with the promise of hearing about an *exciting* life later in the body of the paper.

2. *EXAMPLE A* is problematic for several reasons. First, it doesn't clearly set up the topic, and the information rambles and jumps from one topic to the next with no clearly-defined target. These isolated pieces of information more appropriately belong in a well-developed BODY of the paper. Also *EXAMPLE A* contains sentences with poor variety and structure. It does not **flow** well.

   EXAMPLE C begins well, but then proceeds to wander into unneeded explanation. Once again, the writer tries to explain too much, incorporating information which should come later. The introduction needs to be clear, *to the point* and interesting.

3. *EXAMPLE B* lets you know that you are about to read more information that is *adventurous and interesting and better than any make-believe character you have heard about in a book.* This is a nice transition sentence and it allows the writer to begin to flesh out the high points of Harriet's life.

STAGE TWO: WRITING THE FIRST DRAFT, page 154

Be sure to cover and discuss each drafting tip thoroughly. Most important points are addressed, and they anticipate some common problems students may encounter.

The **Sentence Opening Sheet** is optional for this assignment. However, you might suggest that your students spot check one of their paragraphs using the **SOS**. They could complete a **SOS** for one of the students in their cooperative learning group.

STAGE THREE: REWRITING, page 154

By now, your students should be fairly comfortable using **Checklists** of this sort. Having students *hear* their partners papers before they *read* the paper will help most with numbers 1--5. These questions deal most directly with the paper's content. Have the partners read their papers *aloud* prior to trading.

Numbers 6--9 focus more on proofreading issues and rely on a careful visual scanning of the draft.

Before students write their final draft, it's a good idea to cover the grading sheet or the **SOES** found on page 67 of this guide.

INFORMING CHECKLIST, page 155

STAGE FOUR: PUBLISHING, page 156

Some teachers may elect to have their students use their finished papers as a primary source for short oral presentations. If this is desired, you will need to work with students on hitting only the key points, in an informal speaking manner, as opposed to reading the paper verbatim. This oral paraphrasing or summarizing can actually be a valuable skill to develop.

Suggest that students use colored markers to highlight key sentences and then have them transfer these highlighted areas to note cards. They should then practice speaking only from the notecards.

> Review **The Stack the Deck Writing Process** on pages 4-9 in this guide before teaching this assignment.

STUDENT LEARNING OBJECTIVES

1. The student will write a famous person report about an individual of his/her choice.
2. The student will supply specific information about the person.
3. The student will write at least five paragraphs in the report, each one telling something different about the person.
4. The student will organize the person report according to the format given.
5. The student will write a bibliography, listing the sources of information.
6. The student will include a drawing, an illustration, or a photograph of the person.
7. The student will punctuate correctly.
8. The student will capitalize the correct words.
9. The student will avoid fragments and run-ons.
10. The student's person report will have a cover.

STAGE ONE: PREWRITING, page 157

STUDENT OBJECTIVES AND EVALUATION SHEET-SCORING RUBRIC

See **page 68** in this guide for a copy of the grading sheet.

CHOICE OF A TOPIC, page 158

Before presenting the list of topic choices, check to make sure sources (books, encyclopedias, etc.) are available. Library card catalogs and encyclopedia indexes are helpful. Perhaps your school's media specialist or librarian would be able to help check the source availability. You may have to delete some topic choices or add a few to the list.

Once the list has been checked for source availability, have the students select a first and second choice. This will give you flexibility in distributing the sources so everyone gets his/her own source, rather than fighting over the same book or encyclopedia. Students may select a topic not listed in the text as long as sources are available in the classroom or school library.

BIBLIOGRAPHY INFORMATION, page 159

Encourage the students to record the necessary information right away, rather than postponing it until later. Later might bring disappointment and frustration if the source is missing or checked out. If you or your district uses a different bibliographic format, feel free to substitute it with your class. Be sure to show students where to find copyright dates and to determine the most recent if several dates are listed.

For internet web site bibliographic citations, see Columbia University's web site at www.columbia.edu/cu/cup/cgos/idx_gasic.html>

HELPFUL DRILL: NOTE-TAKING PRACTICE, page 162

Because many students believe that writing a report means copying a few paragraphs from an encyclopedia, note-taking is taught as a skill. Be sure they understand paraphrasing vs. plagiarizing. Point out that FRAGS are OK in notes on Dr. Martin Luther King, Jr.

When they practice taking notes on Amelia Earhart, call on students to volunteer notes they paraphrased. Ask if others wrote a note on the same idea, but used different words to express it. Of course, some words will be duplicated from the text. If you feel your class needs more note-taking practice, simply photocopy an encyclopedia article and instruct them to take 5 notes from it.

HOT TIP: To check on student note-taking, ask a student to read a note back to you; if he/she cannot, then it must be removed. If he/she can read it, then ask for a translation into own words.

HELPFUL DRILL: ORGANIZING THE NOTES, pages 162-163

Explain to the class that Rosa Parks (4) and non-violent protest (6) groups were resorted into the Civil Disobedience group (3) because they are sub-topics. Of course, they could remain separate groups, but then they would need to create their own paragraphs, since they're pretty short., the writer decided to merge them. This is the writer's decision--the students need to make their own best choice in grouping.

If anyone argues that any note is mis-grouped, find out what rationale is used. Discussion of why notes go into which groups is helpful preparation.

Oh yes, show a photograph of Dr. King (or Amelia Earhart or Albert Einstein) during the practice section.

HELPFUL DRILL: CATEGORIZING THE NOTES, pages 164-165

EXERCISE 1:   page 165

Point out the group names selected by Leona for her Einstein report. Some groups may be common for all famous person reports; others are specific to Einstein.

Let students debate which notes belong in which groups; they must be able to defend their choices. Perhaps you may want to place the class in five cooperative learning groups: one for each of Leona's groups. Could be interesting to see which groups claim which notes.

HELPFUL DRILL: COMBINING AND EXPANDING NOTES INTO PARAGRAPHS, pages 165-166

Now comes the reassembly of information into an original and effective written presentation.

The model paragraph on Einstein's theory of relativity uses the **WH word** *which* to combine sentences 17 and 18 and the **glue word** *when* to combine sentences 22 and 28.

EXERCISE 2: page 166

Be sure to have the class share their composed *marriage* paragraphs to reveal the options writers have. Ask the authors to explain why they organize their paragraphs in an order (sequence) and what **glue, WH** connector, or **ING words** they employed to combine notes into sentences.

FAMOUS PERSON REPORT THINK SHEET, pages 167-169

As always, *Open the Deck* provides a **Think Sheet** for your students to jot down information and begin to organize it -- two key functions of the Prewriting Stage. In this unit, there are 2 Think Sheets -- one to list notes from several sources (pages 165-166) and a second to categorize the notes into groups (page 167).

As students use the **1st Think Sheet**, circulate the room to monitor paraphrasing, not plagiarizing.

Before assigning the **2nd Think Sheet**, try **EXERCISE 3** to give the class more grouping practice. Ask for volunteer students who are willing to let the class use their notes for categorizing. Be sure to discuss the various groupings students advocate.

When students group notes, 5 groups are ideal, but not essential. Some lists of notes have 4 groups, 6 groups, or even 7. The number is not essential-- that the groups make sense and hang together is what's important.

Therefore, depending on the number and content of the notes taken, students will make from four to six to seven topics. It is recommended that the teacher meet with each student to approve the **Think Sheet** groupings. This assignment calls for the advanced level thinking skills of categorizing. Some students will need assistance.

STAGE TWO: WRITING THE FIRST DRAFT, page 170

Remind students to begin each paragraph with a topic sentence (controlling idea): a general sentence that contains the topic's SUBJECT from the **Think Sheet.** Additional practice may be needed, using a topic from the Einstein model or from volunteer student work.

For example:

Topic 1   Early interest: **As a young person, Albert had early scientific interests.**

Topic 2   Problems in School: **Most admirers of this genius don't realize that he had problems in school.**

When writing the first draft, students may change the order of their groups; group 1 does not have to become the 1st paragraph. The student-writer must decide on a logical sequence.

INTRODUCTORY AND CONCLUDING PARAGRAPHS, page 170

This is optional: if you think your class can handle adding two more paragraphs to their reports, discuss and model how to do this.

STAGE THREE: REWRITING, page 170

As usual, we provide structured devices for assisting student rewriting. The **checklist** on page 171 follows the same format of peer editing in earlier chapters.

If you assign a **Sentence Opening Sheet**, give them plenty of time to analyze it--this probably is their longest work so far.

FAMOUS PERSON REPORT CHECKLIST, page 171

STAGE FOUR: PUBLISHING, page 172

Provide materials for students to construct a booklet for their report, including all their work: notes, groups, think sheet, checklist, illustration, bibliography, cover. Specify the order you want these parts to go in. Some students may want to place the illustration on the cover. Let them know if that is OK with you. **Note:** If a student copies a picture of a web site, he/she must include a caption that cites the source. (If you have a report/term paper you wrote as a student sometime in the past, bring it in to share.)

Be sure to display the published reports in a prominent place, like the school library, main hall display case, etc. Make a big deal over them. Send some students to other classrooms to read/show off their work. Celebrate their success!!

If you desire another research report assignment, a PLACE REPORT or PRESIDENT REPORT works well. Perhaps you can integrate topics from another curricular area, like science or health. For more ideas about alternate topics, write to us.

The Stack the Deck Writing Program
P.O. Box 429
Tinley Park, Illinois   60477

ON THE SPOT REPORTER
Scoring Rubric--SOES

	Excellent	OK	Needs Improvement

1. Writes an **observation** about a robbery in a video store.

2. **Organizes** the story in a time sequence: before the robbery, during the robbery, and after the robbery scene.

3. Supplies the audience with **specific details**, expanding when necessary.

4. Keeps all the **verbs** in the **past tense** since this a past occurrence.

5. **Varies sentence openings**, not starting every sentence with *The, And then,* or *I.*

6. Uses excellent **word choice.**

7. **Conventions**: spelling, punctuation, and capitalization.

8. **Overall effect** of the paper.

Comment: Grade _____

Name _____ Period _____

JAN'S CHANCE *Student Objectives and Evaluation Sheet*

	Outstanding	Average	Try Again

1. **Combines** sentences using glue words, connectors, colorful words, and verbs to improve sentence fluency.

2. **Varies** the sentence **beginnings.**

3. Keeps **all verbs in the present** tense.

4. Writes an **exemplary ending** that makes the audience want to know more about Jan.

5. **Conventions**: spelling, punctuation, and capitalization.

6. **Overall effect** of the paper.

Comment: Grade_____

ACTION WORD PAPER *Student Objectives and Evaluation Sheet*

	Super	Good	Too Confusing

1. Writes an action word paper, **describing** a **papergirl being chased by a dog**.

2. Uses **ING words** (present participles and gerunds) to improve **sentence fluency,** i. e., *racing down the cobblestone street, growling viciously*, etc.

3. **Organizes** the paper with a beginning, a middle, and an ending.

4. Includes **specific details**, making the story interesting by expanding with journalistic questions.

5. Writes **all verbs** in the **past tense**.

6. **Varies sentence openings**, staying away from *The, And then,* or *I* beginnings.

7. **Conventions**: spelling, punctuation, and capitalization.

8. **Overall effect** of the paper.

Comment:

Grade _____

Name _____ Period _____

BUSINESS LETTER *Student Objectives and Evaluation Sheet*

		Outstanding	Average	Try Again

1. Writes a **business letter** to a
   company, including **six parts:**
   the heading, the inside address,
   the greeting, the body, the closing,
   and the signature.

3. Provides **specific information** in
   the body of the letter.

4. **Organizes** the information in the
   format given.

5. Uses appropriate **tone (voice)** to achieve
   the purpose.

6. **Indents** each new paragraph while
   keeping proper margins.

7. **Conventions**: spelling, punctuation, and
   capitalization.

8. **Overall effect** of the paper.

Comment: Grade_____

Name _____ Period_____

MEMORY PAPER *Student Objectives and Evaluation Sheet*

		Excellent	OK	Needs Improvement

1. Supplies the audience with **specific details**, expanding when necessary.

2. **Organizes** the paper in a limited time sequence.

3. Writes in the **first person**.

4. Keeps all the **verbs** in the **past tense**.

5. **Varies sentence openings**, not starting every sentence with *The, And then,* or *I*.

6. Writes **complete sentences** and **avoids run-ons**.

7. **Conventions**: spelling, punctuation, and capitalization.

8. **Overall effect** of the paper.

Comment: **Grade** _____

Name _____ Period_____

	On Target	On Track	Try Again
1. **Plunges** immediately into the action of the story.			
2. **Organizes** the paper in a time sequence.			
3. Adds **specific details**, using journalistic questions to stretch ideas.			
4. Writes the paper in the **third person**.			
5. **Varies sentence openings**, avoiding repeated *The, And then,* or *I* beginnings.			
6. Keeps all **verbs** in the **present tense**.			
7. Writes **complete sentences** and **avoids run-ons**.			
8. **Overall effect** of the paper.			

Comment: **Grade**_____

Name _____ Period _____

CONTENT PAPER *Student Objectives and Evaluation Sheet*

	Fine Job	So-So	Needs More Work

1. Writes an **expository paper** with the content coming from a writing across the curriculum topic.

2. **Organizes** paper in a logical sequence with an excellent introduction and an exceptional ending.

3. Pulls the best information off the **Think Sheet** and ties it into the paper.

4. Uses **supporting examples** to help the reader get a clear understanding about what the writer is explaining.

5. Writes about **one main idea** in **each paragraph**.

6. **Conventions**: spelling, punctuation, and capitalization.

7. Varies sentence **beginning** and **lengths**.

8. **Overall effect** of the paper.

Comment: Grade _____

Name _____ Period _____

FAMOUS PERSON REPORT *Student Objectives and Evaluation Sheet*

	Great Work	So-So	Must Do Better

1. Writes a famous person **report** about a specific individual.

2. Supplies **specific information** about the famous person.

3. Writes at least **five paragraphs** in the report, each telling something different about the person.

4. **Organizes** the report according to the format given.

5. Writes a **bibliography**, listing the sources of information.

6. Includes a **drawing, illustration,** or a **photograph** of the person.

7. **Conventions:** spelling, punctuation, and capitalization.

8. **Makes a cover.**

9. **Overall effect** of the paper.

Comment: **Grade** _____

Portfolios are becoming a very popular addition to writing classrooms across North America. Why the big push?

Quite simply, portfolios enhance a writing program in two ways. First, they help students recognize their growth in writing. By collecting written work over a period of time, students have evidence of their progress. They may notice an increasing variety of writing genres, improvement in mechanics, more elaborate writing, or better use of dialogue. Generally, students enjoy the feeling of making progress in their writing, and portfolios provide them with a whole "body of work."

Second, portfolios assist teachers, as well. Because we are responsible for assessing our students' progress in writing, we want devices that allows us to do so accurately and confidently. Portfolio collections of student writing provide us with a wider view of student ability than single assessments. Just as the kids can see growth over time, so can we. We also can see areas where more work is needed. By examining actual writing, instead of some standardized test, we can see strengths and weaknesses emerge from the writing pieces.

THE STACK THE DECK WRITING FOLDER

Before a portfolio can be established by a student, he or she first must begin with a writing folder. The writing folder is "temporary holding pen" of all student writing, including prewriting activities, drafts, rewrites, and final copies of any and all assignments, additional ones you assigned, or student-choice writing pieces. Because some kids tend to be less careful with school work than we would like, the writing folder provides them with a safe storage container to collect these precious pieces of writing.

The Stack the Deck Writing Program has ready-made writing folders available to you for this purpose. In addition to providing a safe storage container for students to collect their written work, they also supply your students with other helpful features: a list of correction symbols for revising and proofreading, a place to record all finished pieces of writing, a menu of writing modes, the key traits of effective writing, and the important **Writer's Vocabulary** that is highlighted throughout our textbooks. We formatted our Writer's Folder to be compatible with our composition books. Of course, other writing folders formats may appeal to you.

FROM WRITING FOLDER TO SHOWCASE PORTFOLIO

The Writing Folder also helps students make the bridge between a collection folder and a selection portfolio. Just as professional writers (and artists, photographers, models, architects) select their best pieces of work from their collected body-of-work, so can your students. Because they have collected all their writing into the Writing Folder, they periodically can review this work to determine their "best piece" so far, the "most difficult/frustrating piece," a "work still in progress," and representative pieces in various "modes." The Writing Folder prompts students to make all these selections on the inside cover's "Final Portfolio Selections."

Making selections from the writing folder to the portfolio to showcase student achievement in writing is a critical component of any writing program. First, it places student ownership on their writing as a prominent aspect because they are the ones to make the final selections. Certainly, you as the teacher can conference with them, offering your feedback and opinions on their work. But the final selection belongs to the writers themselves--your students.

How often should your students make selections from their Writing Folder to their portfolios? That is entirely up to you. We only suggest that this selection component of the writing program occur more frequently than just once during the year. Perhaps you can build it into every grading period or before major vacations. Whatever your decision, it is very worthwhile to budget a class period for this selection process and to explain to the kids in advance exactly what you expect them to accomplish.

SELF-REFLECTION PROMPTS

Additionally, **The Stack the Deck Writing Program** believes that student must be given the opportunity and the structure for self-reflection of their writing. An important part of any writer's growth is the ability to think about his or her own writing. For many of your students, self-reflection may not be a natural act, so our program encourages them to practice thinking about their strengths and weaknesses, their growth and frustrations, a part of the portfolio system. By periodically filling in the "Final Portfolio Selections" columns on the inside cover, they are given the opportunity and the structure for increasing their self-reflective powers.

- Where did you get the ideas for this piece?
- What steps did you take to write it?
- Who, if anyone, helped you with it ?
- What, if anything, would you change about it?
- What do you especially like about it?
- Why do you think it's your best piece of writing?
  (from Arts PROPEL, Pittsburgh Public Schools)

Of course, you would not need to assign all of these every time, but rather you could select from the list. Here are a few more of our favorite self-reflection inducers.

- What did you learn about yourself as a writer?
- If you had more time on this assignment, what else would you do?
- If you talked to a younger student about how to be a better writer, what would you pass on that you learned from writing this assignment?

We advise you to be patient with using self-reflective prompts. It will be a new experience for many of your students, and their level of reflective thought, even with a prompt, may be quite low. But stick with them; over the course of the year, young authors can and will improve their ability to think about, and write about, their writing.

PORTFOLIOS

Where should your students place these selected pieces once they have made their choices? They could leave them inside the writing folders, identified in some way. Or they could transfer the selected pieces to another container, the Showcase Portfolio.

Our experience recommends the second approach because kids love the heightened importance of having a portfolio. Some teachers provide the class with construction paper or cardboard to make their own portfolios. Others teachers purchase commercially manufactured portfolio for the class. Ring binder notebooks or colored file folders also could work. A last option is to check with your district's central warehouse for availability and style of possible portfolio containers.

Besides cost and availability, you also want to consider size and shape. Think about the students' writing assignments and published final copies. Is there enough room for them to fit comfortably and easily into the portfolio? And where will you store the portfolios, so that they will be both assessable to the steadiest and also not a nuisance.
Whichever method you pursue, keep in mind that student ownership is very important to a portfolio. The kid should be given the opportunity to decorate and individualize their portfolio. This activity starts the portfolio process off in a popular direction.

FINAL THOUGHTS

No single portfolio system for writing has emerged as the perfect system for everyone. US and Canadian teachers are still experimenting with this new method of assessment. Therefore, we urge you to recognize the need for trial and error, and not to be disappointed when you'll need to make adjustments in your portfolio system. Live and Learn! Let portfolios grow from your writing program so that they become valuable assistants to both you and your students.

CORRECTION SYMBOLS
FOR REVISING AND PROOFREADING

abr .... abbreviation needed or abused

awk .... awkward sentence structure

beginning .... need a *catchy* opening

cap .... capitalization

combine .... **combine** sentences for variety

dm or **mm** .... dangling or misplaced modifier

ending .... need a *pizzazz* ending; not *The End*

expand .... **expand** using journalistic questions

focus .... no clear main idea

frag .... sentence fragment

gap .... a word is missing

^ .... insert a word

log .... not logical

org .... no organization; need a plan

para .... new paragraph needed

punc .... punctuation

? .... confusing

rearrange .... **rearrange** sentence parts

ref .... reference unclear

rep .... repetition; **subtract**

ro .... run-on sentence

seq .... ideas out of order; sequence properly

sp .... spelling

spec .... not specific enough; **expand**

subtract .... **subtract** the yuk

trans .... jumbled ideas; need a transition

var .... vary your sentences; **combine**
                                  and   **rearrange**

vp .... verb power

vt .... verb tense inconsistency

wc .... word choice

yuk .... too wordy; **subtract**

OPEN THE DECK

A step-by-step procedure for writing

by

Tanis Knight and Larry Lewin

The Stack the Deck Writing Program
Tinley Park, Illinois

Acknowledgments

Sniglets: Reprinted with permission of Macmillan Publishing Company from *When Sniglets Ruled the Earth* by Rich Hall. Copyright © 1989 by Not the Network Company, Inc.

We would like to thank the following teachers for their helpful and practical suggestions: Sandra Forkins of the Ridgeland School District in Oak Lawn, Illinois, Bonnie Koontz from St. Joan of Arc School in Toledo, Ohio, and Theresa Wilkie from the Hinsdale School District in Hinsdale, Illinois, and to Theresa Zigmond for editing the original edition of **Open**.

Also, we appreciate Kathy Kupka for proofreading this edition and Joe Koziarski for his illustrations.

ISBN 0-933282-07-9   paperback
ISBN 0-933282-09-5   hardbound

Table of Contents

c

d

f

h

Oral Language Into Writing

You are an expert in the English language. You didn't know that? By the time you were about three years old, you had already learned much about how our language works. By now, you can make thousands and thousands of different sentences. You can understand just as many. Since you can speak the language, you can also learn how to write more effectively. That's what *Open the Deck* is all about.

In this unit you will make many discoveries about your language usage. You will discover skills you already use without realizing that you do. You will become aware of skills that will prove to you how flexible and clever you are in using your language.

These discoveries should make you feel good about your ability to use the English language. Have fun with this unit! Your answers to the questions will seem to come naturally. Be creative and imaginative.

THE LANGUAGE MACHINE

Look at the following four sentences below which are grouped in five columns. Then look at the ten extra words listed after them. Do you realize that from these 30 words it is possible to build thousands of sentences?

Word Chart

	Column 1	Column 2	Column 3	Column 4	Column 5
1.	Bernie	bakes	a	pound	cake.
2.	Katie	fries	two	scrambled	eggs.
3.	Jenny	boils	the	cut	potato.
4.	Lisa	cooks	some	frozen	vegetables.

Extra Words: was, before, by, after, while, and, but, or, who, of

Here are some imaginative sentences made from these 30 words.

1. Bernie bakes the frozen cake.
2. Lisa cooks a scrambled potato.
3. Jenny pounds some frozen vegetables.
4. Katie boils some cut eggs.
5. While baking a cake, Bernie boils some frozen eggs.

Notice the words were chosen randomly from the various columns. Also, the forms of some words were changed.

For example, in sentence 3 of the imaginative sentences, the word, **pounds**, comes from the word, **pound**, in column 4.

Bernie bakes a **pound** cake.

Jenny **pounds** some frozen vegetables.

FUNCTIONAL SHIFT

When you change the form of the word you're using, (e. g., **pound to pounds**) this is called a functional shift. Most of the words in the English language are very flexible in their use. They can shift both their form and function. This is why we can write thousands and thousands of sentences from just 30 words.

WARM-UP ACTIVITY 1

In order for you to see some of the possibilities of this functional shift, look at the following forms of the word **pound**:

Bernie bakes a **pound** cake.	(adjective)
Katie fried a **pound** of potatoes.	(noun)
Lisa **pounds** the steak.	(verb, present)
Bernie **pounded** the aluminum into shape.	(verb, past)
Pounding the counter, Jenny cut some fries.	(present participle)
The eggs, **pounded** by Lisa, were frozen.	(past participle)

Now look at the individual words that we can also get from the word **bakes**.

I **bake**	a **bake** sale	a **half-baked** idea
he **bakes**	a **baker**	a **clambake**
you **baked**	a **bakery**	a **baker's** dozen
baking a cake	a **baked** pie	a **baking** pan
a championship **bake-off**	**unbaked** cookie dough	I'm **baked**

Can you think of other examples for the word **bake**?

WARM-UP ACTIVITY 2

It's your turn to try this technique. Choose one word from columns 2,4,5 on page 1 and come up with different functional shifts for that word. Study the examples you were given for **pound** and **bake**. Notice the different ways the words were used. Remember, get your imagination going.

WARM-UP ACTIVITY 3

You are ready now to make up your own sentences by following the order of the boxes. Pick words from the numbered columns of the word chart on page 1. Use the skill of functional shift to increase the variety of your sentences.

Notice that the last four sentences in this exercise include some of the extra words which were listed below the word chart. (Extra Words = EW in the boxes below.)

Examples:

1	2	3	4	5
Bernie	cooks	some	frozen	vegetables.

1	4	3	2	5
Katie	freezes	two	cooked	potatoes.

1.

1	2	3	4	5

2.

1	4	3	2	5

3.

1	5	1's	4	5

4.

1	2	1

5.

1	2,	2	EW=and	2
4	5			

6.

1	2	3	4	5	EW=but
1	2	3	4	5	

7.

2-ING	3	4	5,	1
2	3	4	5	

8.

3	5	EW=was/were	2	EW=by
1				

Sentence Manipulation

Sentences are collections of short ideas which have been tied together in a neat package. The package often contains many different ideas when we examine it closely. For example, look at this sentence.

Funny Freddy flipped frisbees onto the frozen frog pond.

If you really think about it, this sentence can be broken down into shorter, separate ideas. These ideas are known as kernel ideas because they represent a kernel or start of a sentence. For example, the first *idea* you find is the central idea. For our purposes we state this central idea like this:

1. There is someone named Freddy.

Every time you break down a sentence into its kernels, write the kernels into complete sentences. When necessary, add *There is* or *There are*. Here are the rest of the kernels.

2. Freddy is funny.   **5. There is** a pond.
3. Freddy flipped.   **6.** Frogs live in the pond.
4. There are frisbees.   **7.** The pond is frozen.

Notice that one sentence manages to collect all of these kernel ideas into a single package. It's easy for us to do this. We do it every time we speak.

Good writers also do this, and they practice different ways of packaging kernels into sentences.

BREAKING DOWN SENTENCES INTO KERNELS

EXERCISE 1: On a separate sheet of paper, list all of the kernels or separate ideas in the following sentences. Make the same kind of list which was made for the sample sentence above. Your teacher will work through sentence 1 with the entire class. You might also want to complete this drill as a cooperative learning activity.

1. Your dog wears navy blue army boots and orange suspenders.
2. The evil vampire swooped toward the lovely, young maiden.
3. The green-whiskered troll lived under the creaky bridge.
4. Slim Sampson slipped around the corner and snickered.
5. Wild Wilma waltzed through the whirling water sprinkler.

COMBINING WITH COLORFUL KERNELS

Now that you realize that kernels are found in all sentences, you can combine kernels in many ways. Sometimes, to make your sentence more interesting, you'll want to **expand** with more colorful kernels. You can practice by stretching sentences.

Sentence Stretches

Sentences can be **expanded** by **combining** new kernel ideas. Read the following:

Example:

1. The goat eats poison ivy pudding.
2. The goat is smelly.
3. The goat is old.
4. The poison ivy pudding is spicy.

All of these kernels can be **combined** to make a new, more interesting sentence. One possibility is:

The old, smelly goat eats spicy, poison ivy pudding.

EXERCISE 2: On a separate sheet of paper, see if you can make a new sentence by **combining** the kernels in each sentence below. Use the same sentence combining ideas which you saw in the sample sentence above. Do the first two orally as a group activity.

Example: Felix gobbled turnips.
             The turnips were lumpy.

             Felix gobbled lumpy turnips.

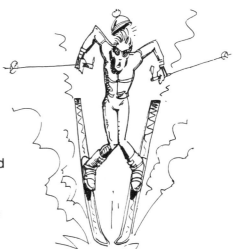

1. My little brother, Seymour, washed his hands in Jell-O. My little brother is brawny.

2. Wally skied warily down the mountain. The mountain was scary.

3. Georgianna yawned, grunted, and scratched her head. Her head was itchy.

4. The wind surfer twisted his board across the wake. The surfer was rugged.

5. The trapeze artist caught her husband.
   The trapeze artist was scrawny.
   The husband was huge.
   The trapeze artist did so happily.

6. Leroy wore tights in the play.
   The tights were leopard-spotted.
   The play was crazy.
   The play was funny.

7. The pig ate grasshoppers.
   The pig was slobbery.
   The grasshoppers were fat.
   The grasshoppers were juicy.

8. Professor U. R. A. Grouch had a nose
   like a hawk.
   The nose was hooked.
   The hawk was fierce.

9. Ulysses won the contest.
   The contest was for squealing
   like a pig.
   He was squealing like Miss Piggy.

10. Herb rides his exercise bike.
    He is muscular.
    He is my uncle.

EXPANDING IDEAS USING JOURNALISTIC QUESTIONS

Any time you decide you want to **expand** your own sentences, you can make the job easier by asking questions about the main idea. For instance, read this short sentence and the question words which come after it.

The Glenview Gophers were defeated.

When?
Why?
How?

The task is to write another sentence in which you **expand** by answering the unanswered questions raised in the original sentence.

On black Saturday the Glenview Gophers were easily defeated because they didn't know the difference between a punt and a pass.

Sentences which contain basic *who* and *what* information can be stretched easily by adding *when, where, why,* and *how* information to the *who--what* kernel.

Question Who? Doer?	Question Does/Did?	Question What?	Questions When? Where? Why? How?
1. The dragon	plays	tennis.	
2. Roughneck Ralph	juggles	golf balls.	

EXERCISE 3: On your own sentence-making sheet, write three different sentences for each set of journalistic questions given. Expand the basic *Who-Doer/Did--What* information you invent with *When, Where, Why,* and *How* information when so requested.

Set 1

Who? Doer?	Did?	What?	When?
Kenyatha	zapped	mosquitoes	last night.

1. _____

2. _____

3. _____

Set 2

Who? Doer?	Did?	What?	Where?
Chris	cracked	corn	in the crib.

1. _____

2. _____

3. _____

Set 3

Who? Doer?	Did?	What?	Why?
Homer	ate	sixty snails	because he liked them.

1. _____
2. _____
3. _____

Set 4

Who? Doer?	Did?	What?	How?
Sylvester	slurps	soup	noisily.

1. _____
2. _____
3. _____

EXERCISE 4: On a separate sheet of paper, **expand** the following sentences by using the journalistic question words after each of them. Here is a list of question words which will be used.

Who? What? When? Where? Why? How?

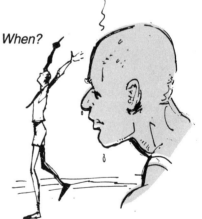

1. My brother Otis grabbed frantically. *What? Why? When?*
2. The figure skater fell. *When? Why?*
3. Angel screams. *Where? Why?*
4. The pigs squealed. *Where? Why? How?*
5. The fragile ice cracked. *Why? Where?*
6. The wolf howls. *When? How?*
7. Sarah listens. *When? Why? How?*
8. Humphrey slapped. *What? Why?*
9. The trees crashed. *Where? When? Why?*
10. Nehemiah lost the race. *How? Why?*

Extra Practice: Why not rearrange your finished sentences? Vary your sentence openings. Begin some of your sentences with your expanded journalistic question phrase. Experiment!

EXERCISE 5: Practice a little more with sentences of your own. Write three sentences about a bullfrog who sings. Each of your sentences should answer at least four of the six journalistic questions. Put your imagination to work.

Here is an example of one sentence which uses the **singing bullfrog** kernel idea.

Example: A nervous, young **bullfrog sings** ballads to his sweetie as the mosquitoes harmonize in the background.

Place a (✓) by the sentence which you think is the most interesting. You will be given an opportunity to share your favorite with the rest of the class. How about this as a cooperative learning activity?

WORD STORAGE BANK

You have probably used a number of colorful words in the sentence **combining** and **expanding** exercises so far. These words can be nouns, verbs, adjectives, or adverbs, but they all stand out because they are not ordinary or hum-drum. They are vivid and interesting.

Many good writers will record such words in a word storage bank for future use in their sentences. At least once a day, it makes good sense to jot down one new word which you really like and might want to use again.

You might want to record the new words in a notebook which you keep at your desk. It's fun to see how many words you can collect in a week, a month, or by the end of the school year.

PUTTING IT ALL TOGETHER

The fun of stretching sentences comes when you see just how unique and different the final results can be. The more you **expand** kernels, the more your readers and you will appreciate your writing. It's time to practice your **writer's vocabulary** skills of sentence **combining** and **expanding**.

Read through the lists with your teacher. Make sure you know the meaning of each word. You will note that the kernel ideas are **Doer** and **Did** words. You will also note that the new words help to answer the question words (journalistic questions) **who**, **what**, **when**, **where**, **why**, and **how**. The extra lines are for your own *creative* words.

KERNEL IDEAS

NEW WORDS

WHO/WHAT			
DOER	**DID**	**WHAT KIND**	**WHEN**
dwarf	giggled	piercing	while he was running
girl	lunged	grouchy	during the practice
ostrich	galloped	blundering	before it's too late
hurricane	smashed	savage	when she finishes
millionaire	sobbed	ancient	after the storm
car	lurched	crimson	_____
rubies	glittered	expensive	_____
rocket	exploded	stocky	
judge	scowled	reckless	**WHERE**
wind	sighed	purple	
singer	bellowed	cute	among the giant redwoods
ape	hung	_____	on the grassy prairie
burglar	tip-toed	_____	near the haunted house
taxi driver	swerved		in the audience
laser beam	reached		over the steep cliff
boy	shouted		
puppy	whined		**WHY**
doctor	operated		because it was time
mountain	erupted		so he could escape
fire	blazed		in order to save his skin
player	volleyed		to get the job done
smoke	belched		_____
clock	ticked		_____
baby	smiled		
floor	creaked		**HOW**
dog	gnawed		merrily,
lady	prayed		abruptly, gently,
fireman	helped		ferociously, angrily,
truant officer	sneaked		typically
_____	_____		_____
_____	_____		_____

EXERCISE 6: See if you can match-up words and phrases with the kernels to make interesting or amusing sentences. Make sure your sentences are unusual. Write six, numbered sentences. In each sentence use words from at least five of the groups given on page 10.

Again, check (✓) the one you like best. Be ready to share it with your classmates. Here are some examples of the kinds of sentences you might make from the word lists. Why not make this a cooperative learning activity?

Examples:

> 1. Angrily, the blundering burglar bellowed as the guard dog gnawed at his leg.

> 2. The ancient ostrich merrily galloped among the giant redwoods.

A WRITER'S VOCABULARY FOR REVISING

Experienced writers practice using a **writer's vocabulary** in order to make their sentences more varied and interesting when they are revising. In the practice exercises, you have used two of the sentence-making skills in your **writer's vocabulary**. You were able to add more words to **expand** the sentences. You also were able to **combine** several shorter sentences to make a new sentence.

Later in this book you will learn another skill to increase your **writer's vocabulary**. The trick is to keep practicing these skills in your own writing, especially in revising a first draft.

Writer's Vocabulary

Combining

and

Expanding

11

COMMAS IN A SERIES

Sometimes you may be building sentences by combining kernels all of which relate to the same thing. For instance, look at these kernels:

Kernels:

1. Loki is a dog.   **3.** Loki is snarling.
2. Loki is tiny.   **4.** Loki is man-eating.

Loki is a tiny, snarling, man-eating dog.

As you can see, the kernels that describe the dog are listed in a series in the new sentence. In a case like this, these words must be separated by commas. A comma is placed *after* each word except the last one.

EXERCISE 7: Combine the kernels listed to form a new sentence. Separate, with commas, all the words which describe the same thing or relate to the same thing. Do the first two as a group activity.

1 . Leon, the elephant, wears socks.
The socks are old.
The socks are smelly.

2 . We gave my sister jellyfish.
The jellyfish were pale pink.
The jellyfish were delicate.
The jellyfish were friendly.

3 . The wolf's teeth were pointed.
The teeth were yellow.
The teeth glistened in the moonlight.

4 . Larry trains alligators.
The alligators are small.
The alligators are lively.
The alligators are hungry.

5 . His skis were in the closet.
His skis were brand new.
His skis were red.
His skis were for cross country.

You have just practiced using the rule of punctuation which is stated below:

COMMA RULE 1

In a sentence, words in a series, except the last word, must be followed
by a comma.

A sentence which follows this rule could look like this:

Her teeny, weenie, yellow, polka-dotted bikini was expensive.

PUNCTUATION RULES FOR YOUR NOTEBOOK

Set aside in your notebook three pages for punctuation rules. Write the new
comma rule you have just learned and a sample sentence to show how it is used.
As you learn new rules in the future, add them to your punctuation rules sheets.

EXERCISE 8: On a separate sheet of paper, see if you can write five sentences
of your own which follow the same sentence pattern which is modeled just above.
In other words, use at least three descriptive words in a series in each sentence.
Be sure you follow the correct comma rule.

USING WRITING TRAITS
TO IMPROVE YOUR COMPOSITIONS

Writing involves many different skills. When you read something that
is written well, you are experiencing a final product that displays the criteria
or (traits) of successful writing combined into one, effective package.
Even though a
writer uses several
of these traits
in combination,
sometimes it's
helpful to separate
the traits out and talk
about them individually.

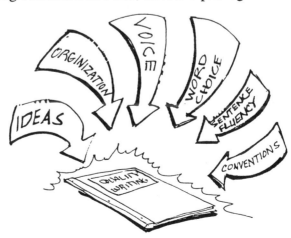

Here are six criteria or traits which most teachers agree should appear in high quality writing.

IDEAS Does my writing have something important to say? Are the ideas clear and compelling?

ORGANIZATION Are my ideas organized well? Is it easy to follow from one idea to another? Do I use paragraph structure and transitions to move the reader along?

VOICE Does this paper sound like me? Can I hear the voice and honest personality of the writer?

WORD CHOICE Have I selected vocabulary words which make the writing easier to picture? Did I choose just the right words to describe or explain something?

SENTENCE FLUENCY Do my sentences flow smoothly when I read them? Have I used a variety of sentence lengths, types and beginnings?

CONVENTIONS Does my writing show a mastery of common spelling, punctuation and capitalization rules? Is it easy to read and written or typed neatly?

Many times teachers or schools or even states will use the traits listed above (or similar traits) to evaluate student writing. For this reason, it makes sense to think about and practice each one.

Throughout *Open the Deck,* we will emphasize various traits and weave them into the chapters. You will be able to work through helpful drills to help you feel more confident using each trait. Most importantly, the major writing assignments in this book will give you a chance to apply the traits you've learned.

Major Writing Assignment

On the Spot Reporter

A good writer is a thinker, a person who knows his subject. Before you begin to write a paragraph, you should think through your subject and jot down ideas to see if you really know enough about it.

Ask yourself the journalistic questions **who**, **what**, **when**, **where**, **why**, and **how** just as the professional writers do. **Expand** each idea to make it as specific as possible. This prewriting activity is one of the keys to becoming an excellent writer.

STAGE ONE: PREWRITING

STUDENT LEARNING OBJECTIVES

1. The student will write a short observation of a scene and tell what happens during the robbery.
2. The student will **expand** some of his sentences to make them more interesting. Tell **who**, **what**, **when**, **where**, **why**, and **how**.
3. The student will use commas to separate descriptive words found in a series.
4. The student will write the observation in past tense.
5. The student will use effective **word choice.**

HELPFUL DRILL RELATED TO WORD CHOICE

The first writing trait we will explore is **WORD CHOICE**. As you might expect, word choice relates to vocabulary. As you write, you want to pick words or vocabulary that are interesting and really help the reader "see" what you are describing. These words don't have to be just adjectives. Often you will want to select just the right noun or verb or adverb to make a sentence come alive.

EXERCISE 9: The author of the paragraph on the next page has a problem. She has used lots of dull, ho-hum words in her sentences. For this reason, the paragraph isn't very interesting to read. She needs to demonstrate a better use of **WORD CHOICE**. Rewrite the paragraph on your own paper. Replace each italicized, bold word with a better one. If you want to use more than one word, that's fine too. If you see a blank line, fill it in with your own word.

Example: Brett **walked** to the mail box and **took out** the _____ envelope with his semester grades inside.

15

New Sentence with better WORD CHOICE:

> Brett **shuffled** to the mail box and **painfully withdrew** the **oversized, mustard-colored** envelope with his semester grades inside.

PRACTICE PARAGRAPH: FAILED FIELD TRIP

The field trip bus driver *moved* into her seat and turned on the ignition key.

The bus engine made a _____ sound and the engine *came* to life.

Soon the yellow *box* on wheels was _____ down the road, filled with

fifty _____ students and two *tired* teachers. Overhead, the sky looked like

_____. Outside the bus windows, _____cows

chewed their breakfast and stared at the *noisy bus*. They stopped chewing when the

bus made a *loud noise*. A **black** cloud of smoke *came out of* the back of the bus,

and the wheels _____ to a stop.

EXERCISE 10:

Each phrase below tells you about the topic and action of a sentence to be written. Use this information to write a new sentence. Use at least three interesting word choices to help make the sentence easy to visualize.

Example: girl riding her bike

> The **gangly** four year-old pushed off on her big sister's **shiny two wheeler** and **lurched** down the road.

1. hang glider coming in for a landing
2. rabbit trying to hide from a hawk
3. a spy climbing over a fence
4. volleyball player hitting the winning serve
5. a horse jumping over a fence

WRITING PROMPT--TOPIC

Now it's time to begin your major writing piece for this unit. Pretend that you watched a robbery take place in a video store near your home. This happened a month ago. Now the police have arrested the alleged robbers. They need a very clear and vivid description of what you saw. It is important that you **expand** your sentences to include as much **who, what, when, where, why,** and **how** information as possible. You will be working from the kernel notes given below.

For this project, fill out the **Think Sheet** provided by your teacher. Use your imagination! Stretch ideas! Write your responses to each part of the **Think Sheet** on your own paper.

Kernel Notes

1. Store was crowded.
2. The holidays were coming soon.
3. Store was big.
4. Store owner was busy.
5. Employees were busy.
6. Robbers entered quietly.

7. Robbers looked strange.
8. Robbers pulled out guns.
9. All people panicked.
10. Robbers got nervous.
11. Robbery was stopped in a surprising way.

ON THE SPOT REPORT THINK SHEET

Before the robbery:

1. In what kind of store did the action take place?

_____

2. What were the holiday types of sounds, sights, colors, or smells that you experienced? List at least three details. Be clear in your wording. **Expand!**

   a. _____

   _____

   b. _____

   _____

   c. _____

   _____

3. How did the store owner, the employees and/or the customers act? How could you tell that they were busy before the robbers entered? **Expand!**

   a. Store owner_____

   _____

   _____

   b. Employees_____

   _____

   _____

   c. Customers_____

   _____

   _____

During the robbery:

4. How did the robbers first act when they entered the store? Tell your audience specifically how they entered. **Expand!**

_____

_____

_____

5. How many robbers were there?_____

6. It is noted that the robbers looked strange. Tell us how they looked. Use specific examples. **Expand!**

_____

_____

7. What did the robbers do? **Expand!**

_____

_____

8. Give some clear examples of how certain people panicked as the robbers pulled out their guns. **Expand!**

_____

_____

_____

End of the unsuccessful robbery attempt:

9. Finally, we know the robbery attempt ended in some unusual way. Think about the ending carefully. Describe how the incident ended. Use your imagination. **Expand!**

_____

_____

STAGE TWO: WRITING THE FIRST DRAFT

With your **Think Sheet** completed, you have all the information you need to write a short description of the robbery scene. It may be easier for you to think of writing about the action in three paragraphs:

1. the store **before** the robbery took place

2. **as** the robbers moved into action

3. the scene **at the end** of the robbery

Reminder: Since this robbery attempt took place over a month ago, remember to keep all your verbs in the past tense.

GUIDELINES FOR WRITING THE FIRST DRAFT

As a basic guideline, try to organize your paragraphs on your first draft or sloppy copy like this:

- Write quickly. Handwriting doesn't have to be your neatest at this stage.

- *Guess and Go Spelling.* Guess how to spell hard words. Circle them to check later. Then go on.

- Not all parts must be perfect. Pay attention to ideas first. You can correct, spell, and punctuate later. You cannot do a good job on both ideas and mechanics at the same time.

To make your story easier to work on later:

- Write in pencil.

- Skip every other line.

- Number each sentence on the sloppy copy.

As you begin to write, you can use the **Think Sheet** as a guideline to help organize three paragraphs. Here are some tips:

PARAGRAPH ONE

- Use questions one through three on your **Think Sheet** as organizers.

- Be sure to use lots of details to help your reader be able to picture what you are describing. Carefully think about your word choice.

- **Expand** and **combine** sentences.

PARAGRAPH TWO

- Use questions number four through eight to describe the beginning of the robbery. Help your audience to see what the robbers looked like and how they acted. Also don't forget to describe the actions of the customers.

- Focus on action in this paragraph. What words will best convey this action?

PARAGRAPH THREE

- Look at number nine on your **Think Sheet** and make the third paragraph the ending for your scene.

- Remember that the robbery ends in some surprising way.

- Make sure there is a good conclusion and that the action does not just stop abruptly with the words *The End*. Wrap up all the loose ends.

STAGE THREE: REWRITING

With the three paragraphs on your sloppy copy, you have a good start towards a finished product. The final draft needs to be polished so that it is something you can really be ready to publish.

On the next page is an **Editor's Checklist** to help with your rewriting tasks. A classmate or your editing partner will fill out the sheet and sign it after he or she reads your paper.

In order to really hear your ideas, it is OK if you or your partner reads your paper aloud softly. Use a 12 inch voice. That is, you shouldn't be able to hear the voice more than one foot away from the speaker.

Your teacher might also divide the class into cooperative learning groups to help each of you edit your draft.

Writer's Name_____

Editor's Name_____

ON THE SPOT REPORTER CHECKLIST

1. What did you like **best** about this observation? Back up your ideas with sentences from the writer's paper that you thought were especially good.

_____

_____

2. What descriptive words or phrases that the writer **expanded** really helped you see this robbery? List as many as you can.

_____

_____

_____

3. Where does the writer need to **expand** with more specific information?

_____

_____

4. How did the writer wrap up all the pieces of the observation in the ending? What other ways could she have ended the observation?

_____

_____

5. What's your number one suggestion to really help improve this piece of writing? Write a complete sentence telling your ideas and list examples to back up what you say.

_____

_____

_____

USING YOUR EDITOR'S CHECKLIST

Once you receive your **Editor's Checklist** back, you should read it carefully. Then rewrite your rough draft using the suggestions you think are the best, plus your own new ideas.

You might also want to review the objectives from the grading sheet (scoring rubric) you received in the prewriting stage. As you rewrite your final copy, don't forget to check your speling(*oops*), spelling, punctuation, and capitalization.

STAGE FOUR: PUBLISHING

When everyone has finished his robbery scene, chances are that many of these compositions will be really exciting. Be prepared to share some of your writing orally with the class. Which descriptions would make the most exciting TV or movie scenes?

How about some Oscar-winning performances acting out your scene for your classmates?

Oral Language into Writing

NEVER HEARD BEFORE SENTENCES

You are already very savvy about the sentence patterns of our language. You know how language works without having been taught about this. You hear ideas that you have never heard before and understand them. Why? **You're a walking grammar machine.** Let's prove this.

Sentences follow a common order and have a limited number of patterns. Even though you have never heard the following sentence patterns before, you will understand their *ridiculous* meanings because of your knowledge of language.

WARM-UP ACTIVITY 1

Read the following sentences and explain what they mean in your own words. Do this orally with the entire class.

1. Blind bats never save coupons even though they often shop at McMilly's Supermarket.

2. Donnie Dingdong was last spotted leap-frogging over telephone poles in North Cupcake, Vermont.

3. Seventy-five bluish grey seals board a jet to vacation on a tropical island during the winter months.

4. Jerome juggled jelly jars while Angie mistakenly mixed mushrooms in Salvador's soup.

5. Did they know there was a tax on purple shoelaces and frying pans in Lunchbox, Louisiana?

WARM-UP ACTIVITY 2

Make up three never heard before sentences. Put a star next to your best one, and read it to a partner(s).

Sentence Manipulation

You learned in **Unit 1** that the combining of kernel ideas is the beginning of any writing. Nearly all sentences are made of **idea words** and **glue words**.

Idea words in a sentence name the Doer and the Does/Did. They are nouns and verbs. Idea words also include colorful words which stretch the content--adjectives and adverbs. They answer the journalistic questions **who**, **what**, **when**, **where**, **why**, and **how**.

Glue words (like conjunctions) are words that connect or glue together different ideas to build sentences. In the following example, the **glue word** is **boldfaced**.

> **After** winning the spelling contest, Aretha received
> an award and whooped wildly.

Let's take a look at a new family of **glue words**. You can learn to use them to build better sentences.

Glue Words--Subordinating Conjunctions

after	because	since	whenever
although	before	so that	where
as	even though	though	wherever
as if	if	unless	while
as long as	in order that	until	
as though	in order to	when	

EXERCISE 1: Now it's time for you to get into the sentence building business again. Combine these small sentences into fancier ones, using **glue words** (subordinating conjunctions) in the middle. Follow these three rules:

- use as many different **glue words** as you can. (Don't use any one more than twice.)
- remember to use capital letters and punctuation.
- underline the **glue word** in the new sentence.

1. The floor is slippery.
   It was washed.

2. Gus broke his nose.
   He played rough.

3. I will give less homework this evening.
   Everyone must finish his problems.

4. Uncle Joe bought stinky cheese.
   He hates cheese.

5. Everyone must finish his job on time.
   We can enjoy a delicious Thanksgiving dinner.

6. Barney's motorcycle skidded.
   A car leaked oil.

7. There is a giant, squishy puddle.
   It rains.

8. Mabelline shouts.
   She is angry.

9. Ms. Tarlov teaches school.
   She loves children.

10. Eddy is lonely.
    He has many friends.

11. I like hot chili.
    It spices up my tacos.

12. Esther swam a mile.
    She rode her bike twenty miles.

13. There is a crack in the foundation.
    The building is new.

14. The snoring snake slept.
    The sun was hot.

15. Millie acts.
    She won the math contest.

VARYING SENTENCE OPENINGS WITH GLUE WORDS

You should know that you can also **combine** ideas by writing sentences which begin with **glue words**. This will enable you to vary your sentence beginnings instead of always starting sentences with *The, I, And then*.

Here are some examples:

1. *Because* Regional slipped, he fell on his ear.
2. *If* Kathy will help, Donnie can come to the party.
3. *Even though* the Titans lost, the team played well.
4. *Unless* Calvin climbs down, Hobbies will swallow a fish.
5. *As long as* the deer runs, the arrow will not find its mark.

USING COMMAS TO SET OFF A CLAUSE

You may combine two sentences using a **glue word** either at the beginning of the sentence or in the middle. If you place it at the beginning, you will need a comma. If the **glue word** is used in the middle of the sentence, you will not need a comma.

The rule which explains the need for this comma is written below:

COMMA RULE 2

When a sentence begins with a **glue word,** put a comma *after* the first part of the sentence **which is actually a dependent clause.**

Here is a sentence which follows this rule:

While <u>Melba cut carrots,</u>   <u>I sliced tomatoes.</u>
GLUE WORD   1st PART   COMMA   and 2nd PART

Make up your own sentence which illustrates this rule. Follow this model pattern when you write your own sentence.

EXERCISE 2:   Combine these sentences using **glue words** at the beginning of each. Be sure to add a comma in the correct place. Do not use the same **glue words** (subordinating conjunctions) more than twice. Punctuate correctly.

1. The picnic had been postponed.
   Dawn won the pie-eating contest.

2. Jay gets the job.
   He will give his brother Paul a raise.

3. Dora eats oysters.
   She then drinks a quart of chocolate milk.

4. Santa Claus slid down the chimney.
   Jenny tacked up her stocking.

5. Everyone gets a chance to win the prize.
   I will call on each class member in turn.

6. Donna goes.
   I will track her down.

7. Aretha is tall and quick.
   She is a star basketball player.

8. The dishes are dirty.
   Cousin Billie must wash them.

9. The parakeet sings.
   The cat licks his chops.

10. The accident took place.
    Main St. intersects Columbus Drive.

11. The glue was weak.
    The chair came apart when Larry sat down.

12. Nancy is dead broke.
    She is happy.

13. The fly crashed into the web.
    The spider was waiting.

14. Christine is hungry.
    She gobbles popcorn.

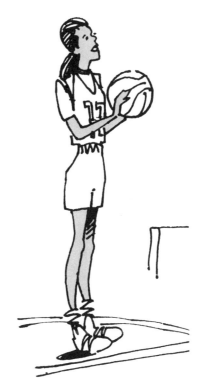

MORE PRACTICE COMBINING WITH GLUE WORDS

EXERCISE 3: Instead of writing short, choppy sentences, you are going to practice combining short sentences into one good sentence.

Example: The costume party began.
               I put on my fangs.
               They were vampire fangs.

By using a glue word at the **beginning** of the sentence, these ideas can be combined in at least two different ways.

   1. **Before** the costume party began, I put on my vampire fangs.

   2. **Before** I put on my vampire fangs, the costume party began.

Notice the shift in meaning in these two sentences. Also, notice that the writer placed a comma in the right spot. Do the same with the sentences on the next page. Combine three sentences into one. Punctuate properly. Use each **glue word** at least once. Complete the first two as a group activity. You must be able to explain how your choice of a particular **glue word** affects the sentence's meaning.

TIME GLUE WORDS   MEANING

after	=	as soon as; following the time that
as	=	at the same time that; while
before	=	in advance of the time when
since	=	after the time when
until	=	up to the time that
when	=	at the time that
while	=	as long as; during the time that

1. The game was on Thursday.
It began at four o'clock.
The umpire rubbed up the baseballs.

2. Meg brushes her teeth.
She brushes them in the bathroom
She eats breakfast

3. Jake passed his exam.
It was a science exam.
Jake was promoted to the 8th grade.

4. The concert was in progress.
The fans rocked in their seats.
Their seats were in the stadium.

5. The wind blew.
It stirred up the dust.
There was dust on the field.

6. Allan moved.
He moved to a new apartment.
Allan rented a U-Haul trailer.

7. Niki bought a car.
The car was a 1968 Volkswagen.
She went to many used car lots.

8. The storm was terrifying.
Lucas and Madi waited in the barn.
The storm ended.

9. Aileen washed the pots and pans.
She and Paul were in the kitchen.
Paul emptied the dishwasher.

10. Bo retrieved the ball.
The ball was torn.
He dropped it at his master's feet.

UNCOMBINING SENTENCES

Now that you're becoming a pro at sentence combining, let's see if you remember what little kernels look like.

EXERCISE 4: Uncombine the following sentences to make them into short sentences. The first one is modeled for you.

1. After Brett Favre passed the ball, he was knocked down.

    a. Brett Favre passed the ball.
    b. He was knocked down.

2. Even though we recycle glass, we still have too much garbage.
    a.
    b.

3. When it rains, it pours.
    a.
    b.

4. Cinda will help build the fort up if Kendra finds the hammer and saw.
    a.
    b.

5. Her party was excellent because the birthday cake fell onto the floor.
    a.
    b.

COMBINING AND EXPANDING IDEAS INTO A PARAGRAPH

Here's a chance to practice your new skills with **glue words**. First, study the six kernels and the **glue words** given. Then look at how one student combined them into a short paragraph.

Kernel Ideas	Glue Words	Meaning	
1. There is a brother.	because	=	for the reason that
2. There is a sister.	before	=	earlier
3. There is a skateboard.	while	=	as long as
4. There is a fight.	if	=	on the condition that
5. There is a mother.	unless	=	except if
6. The mother is sad.			

31

Double Trouble

1. Because Ann had a skateboard, her brother wanted one. **2.** He tried out hers **before** buying his own. **3. While** Kelvin tried it, Ann noticed him zooming down the street. **4.** She didn't like this and decided to chase him. **5.** She hopped on Kelvin's ten-speed bicycle. **6.** She screamed that she would ride his bike through Rocky Creek **unless** he gave her the skateboard back. **7.** Kelvin headed down the hill with Ann's pedaling after him. **8.** At the bottom she caught him. **9.** Both jumped off and started screaming like monkeys wanting a banana. **10.** Their mother, coming home from work, saw them arguing. **11.** She felt sad, knowing that she'd have to take away both the skateboard and the bicycle. **12. If** they had just been more understanding, this fight could have been avoided.

Notice how the writer used her imagination. She explained what started the fight, how it happened, and how it ended.

EXERCISE 5: Now it's your turn. Here are six different sentences for you. Use the five **glue words** to write your own paragraph. Don't be afraid to use your imagination and **expand** as the writer of **Double Trouble** did. Expand with new information to the story to make it better--more exciting to read.

How about completing this as a cooperative learning activity?

Kernel Ideas	Glue Words
1. There is a little boy.	because
2. There is a little girl.	before
3. There is a spelling bee.	while
4. There is a contest.	if
5. There is a teacher.	unless
6. The teacher is happy.	

CHANGING MEANINGS BY POSITIONING GLUE WORDS

Deciding where to put in a **glue word** can make all the difference in the world. Watch!

Example: Mario washes the grapes **before** he shoves the bunch into his mouth.

In this sentence Mario at least had the good sense to wash the grapes *first*. The **glue word** in the middle of the sentence tells the reader this.

What happens to the meaning of the sentence if the same **glue word** is positioned at the beginning of the sentence?

Example: **Before** Mario washes the grapes, he shoves them into his mouth.

In this sentence not only is Mario greedy, but he doesn't even care if dangerous pesticide spray might be on the grapes. That's a big difference.

The position of the **glue word** changes the meaning of the sentence. Mario may become *sick* Mario in the second sentence.

EXERCISE 6: Have fun discussing the different meanings of these sentences.

1 . Wanda boils frog teeth in her kettle **unless** the moon turns red.

   Unless Wanda boils frog teeth in her kettle, the moon turns red.

2 . A lonesome boy weeps by the pond **as long as** the other kids won't play with him.

   As long as the lonesome boy weeps by the pond, the other kids won't play with him.

3 . Kelly tosses bananas to Frank **whenever** Frank acts like a chimpanzee.

   Whenever Kelly tosses Frank bananas, Frank acts like a chimpanzee.

EXERCISE 7: Now you change the meanings of these sentences by moving the **glue words**.

1. Ms. Ramirez drives to the gas station before her car runs out of gas.

2. Mr. Chillywinds lights a fire in his fireplace after he peers down the chimney looking for bats.

3. Whenever the Smithsons on Prairie Chicken Court have a party, the neighbors living on Prairie Chicken Court close their windows.

As you can see, using **glue words** at the beginning or the middle of a sentence really gives you control over that sentence. Now you know how to use **glue words** to communicate clearly to your audience.

Combining Tricks

As you know by now, writing follows a step-by-step process. ***Open the Deck*** uses a four step process to help you improve your writing abilities:

1. prewriting
2. writing the first draft--sloppy copy
3. rewriting and editing
4. publishing

Can you explain what you do in each step?

STAGE ONE: PREWRITING

STUDENT LEARNING OBJECTIVES

1. The student will use all four sentence combining tricks.
2. The student will use proper punctuation.
3. The student will invent an original ending to the story.

USING WRITING TRAITS TO IMPROVE YOUR COMPOSITIONS

Remember that in **Unit One** we talked about how effective writers can focus on certain "writing traits" to improve their work. In that unit we discussed making just the right "word choice."

In **Unit Two**, we will introduce another trait. This is the idea of using **SENTENCE FLUENCY**. Although this may sound complicated, all it means is that when you read your work, the sentences seem to flow naturally--with a good rhythm.

To achieve this natural flow, there are several methods you might want to try. For example, you want to be sure that all your sentences are not the same length. Are some shorter; some longer? If yes, usually this will help the writing seem more like natural speech.

In addition, you can also work to vary your sentence beginnings and combining patterns. With the sentence manipulation you have been working on, you have already done this. First, you practiced combining smaller choppy sentences into longer ones. You also used descriptive words to s--t--r--e--t--c--h some sentences. Finally, in this unit, you have been using **glue words** to begin some sentences with clauses.

WRITING PROMPT

You are now ready to use your fancy sentence combining skills to write a story about a new baseball player facing a big pressure. The story has already begun, but it has two major problems:

- It has only little, boring sentences.
- It has a beginning and a middle, but no ending.

Read the story **Jan's Chance** aloud with your class listening for possible ways to combine the sentence sets. Remember that you have many combining tricks you can use.

- Glue words, page 26
- Colorful words in a series, page 5

Jan's Chance

1. It is warm.
2. It is sunny.
3. It is springtime.

4. Jan thinks of softball.
5. Jan discards the idea of running track.
6. She decides to try out for the softball team.

7. Will she make the team?
8. Will she miss the cut in the try-outs?
9. The first game of the season is under way.
10. She has made the team.
11. She is on the bench.

12. Jan yells encouragement to the starters.
13. She jumps up and down with excitement.
14. She moans when the close calls go against the team.

15. The close game is in the last inning.
16. The score is tied.

17. Our Generals load the bases.
18. The next two batters strike out.

19. The coach looks down the bench.
20. His eyes stop when they reach Jan.

21. He tells her to get a bat.
22 He tells her to bring 'em in.

JAN'S CHANCE THINK SHEET

To help you plan your story, fill out this **Think Sheet**. Remember, you may change the sentences in your final copy. This sheet should help you get started.

1. Which group of sentences will you combine with **glue words**?
   sentences _____

2. Which group will you combine with **verbs**? sentences _____

3. Which group will you combine with connectors--**and, but, or**?
   sentences _____

4. Which group will you combine with **colorful words**? sentences _____

5. What type of ending will you write to make this story more interesting? Here are some possible choices: happy, surprising, sad, mysterious.

STAGE TWO: WRITING THE FIRST DRAFT---sloppy copy

DRAFTING RULES

Here are some tips to help you write your first draft of **Jan's Chance**.

- *Guess and Go* spelling.
  Special Tip: circle any word(s) that you think might be mispelled, *oops*, misspelled.

- Write quickly.

- Your draft doesn't have to be perfect. Remember, ideas first, then mechanics.

- Write in pencil.

- Skip lines

- Number sentences

- Write on the front side of paper only.

Remember a first draft is just your first try--it doesn't have to be perfect; it can be sloppy.

STAGE THREE: REWRITING

USING THE SENTENCE OPENING SHEET TO REVISE

Now that you have finished your rough draft of **Jan's Chance**, it may be a good time to take a brief break from your work before you begin to revise the draft. In this next activity, you will be introduced to a powerful tool to help you revise your first working drafts. This tool is called the "Sentence Opening Sheet." It is helpful for lots of reasons, but it is particularly good if you want to work on your sentence variety and fluency.

So complete this exercise, and then you will be ready to revise your own work.

EXERCISE 8: In **The Colfax Crushers** paragraph (**below**), the writer included many short, choppy sentences. Read the story aloud. Then use our special **Sentence Opening Sheet** to help you analyze and rewrite this first draft using your **writer's vocabulary**.

The Colfax Crushers

1. There was a quarterback at Colfax Middle School. **2.** The quarterback was in seventh grade. **3.** The quarterback was scrawny. **4.** The quarterback had a weak line. **5.** The green quarterback wasn't very good. **6.** He threw passes. **7.** The passes were intercepted. **8.** He ran the ball. **9.** He was sacked. **10.** He was teased. **11.** His team lost. **12.** It was summer. **13.** The quarterback worried about the next season. **14.** The quarterback worked out. **15.** The quarterback drank thirty-two milk shakes a day. **16.** He put on weight. **17.** The quarterback rode his bike. **18.** From his bike he looked for strong guys. **19.** He looked for big guys. **20.** He looked for fast guys. **21.** He looked for guys who had just been promoted. **22.** He looked hard. **23.** He found help. **24.** It was fall. **25.** Things were better. **26.** Points were scored. **27.** The team the quarterback recruited beat everyone. **28.** They were known as **The Colfax Crushers**.

Now you will learn a handy-dandy way to rewrite a paragraph using a **Sentence Opening Sheet** to analyze your work.

After composing a first draft, the writer listed her first four words per sentence in column 1. In column 4 she listed the number of words included with each sentence.

Study the completed **SOS** sheet for columns 1 and 4 on the next page. What do you notice about each column?

Sentence Opening Sheet

VAR	First 4 Words Per Sentence	Special	HE_____ Verbs	VAR # of Words
1.	There was a quarterback			8
2.	The quarterback was in			6
3.	The quarterback was scrawny			4
4.	The quarterback had a			6
5.	The green quarterback wasn't			6
6.	He threw passes			3
7.	The passes were intercepted			4
8.	He ran the ball			4
9.	He was sacked			3
10.	He was teased			3
11.	His team lost			3
12.	It was summer			3
13.	The quarterback worried about			7
14.	The quarterback worked out			4
15.	The quarterback drank thirty-two			8
16.	He put on weight			4
17.	The quarterback rode his			5
18.	From his bike he			8
19.	He looked for big			5
20.	He looked for fast			5
21.	He looked for guys			9
22.	He looked hard			3
23.	He found help			3
24.	It was fall			3
25.	Things were better			3
26.	Points were scored			3
27.	The team the quarterback			7
28.	They were known as			7

COLUMN 1--FIRST FOUR WORDS PER SENTENCE--*VARIETY*

After studying Column 1, did you notice that by writing the first words of each sentence in column form, it is then easy to see if the same words have been used over and over again as sentence openings?

Together, discuss the following questions about the sentence openings from **The Colfax Crusher**:

1. Do too many of the sentences start the same way, with *The quarterback,* for example? If too many of the sentence openings sound the same, how could you **combine** them to have more variety?

2. Do any of the sentences start with **glue words**? If not, you might use a **glue word** to begin a sentence and provide more variety.

3. Do all of the sentences begin with a capital letter? Be sure to double check.

COLUMN 4--NUMBER OF WORDS PER SENTENCE--*VARIETY*

When you analyze the number of words per sentence in Column 4, first look to see if the writer included too many short, choppy sentences. If so, try **combining** some of the ideas to make better sentences.

YOUR TURN

As a class project, with your teacher doing the actual writing, rewrite **The Colfax Crushers** story by **combining** some of the shorter sentences.

Remember, you "now" have many ways to **combine** sentences:

Before you start, you might want to read the sentences aloud again, and decide which ones can be **combined**. List their numbers together on a planning sheet before you start combining. Can you combine the 28 short, choppy sentences into just 10 longer ones? How about 9? 8? 7 sentences?

SOS TO THE RESCUE

Now it's time to see how well your own first draft of **Jan's Chance** turned out. You are going to use the same type of Sentence Opening Sheet you just used in **The Colfax Crusher** exercise.

Your teacher will give you a copy of the SOS to fill in.

Sentence Opening Sheet

Name_____

First Four Words Per Sentence	Special	Verbs	# of Words

COLUMN 1

In column 1, list the first four words of each sentence. Ask yourself the following questions about column 1:

1. Do too many of the sentences repeat the same openings, with *Jan*, for example? If too many of your sentence openings sound the same, which sentence(s) can you **combine** to vary your openings? Or could you **rearrange** the sentences?
2. Do any of your sentences begin with **glue words**? If not, maybe you can **combine** some sentences and begin with a **glue word**.
3. Do all of your sentences begin with a capital letter? If not, you forgot to capitalize the first word of a sentence, so go back to your story and fix it.

COLUMN 2

Skip column 2 for this assignment.

COLUMN 3

Record the verb(s) from each sentence in column 3. Identifying verbs can be a difficult task. If you have problems picking out verbs, write the expression **HE____** above the verb column. Every time you select a verb to list in column 3, read *that* word after the expression **HE____**. If it makes sense, it is probably a verb.

Examples: He_____
             He <u>swimming</u>.   *Swimming* is not a verb in this sentence.
                              Why?
                              The sentence does not make sense.
             He <u>runs</u>.   *Runs* is the verb. Right?

Ask yourself the following questions after completing column 3:

1. Do any of my sentences have three verbs? If so, go back to the story and see if you punctuated correctly.
2. Are all the verbs present tense (Does)? If not, go back to your draft and change the past tense verbs into present tense.

COLUMN 4

Skip column 4 for now. You'll be working on it later in this book.

Now make changes on your first draft--*sloppy copy*--based upon your **SOS** sheet findings.

GETTING BY WITH A LITTLE HELP FROM MY FRIEND

You might have made changes on your first draft after analyzing columns 1 and 3 on your **Sentence Opening Sheet**.

Another way of improving your writing is to get help from a classmate. All professional writers realize that it's a smart idea to ask an opinion from someone about what they have written. The person they trust to give them help is called their editor.

Your teacher will provide you with an editor who will offer you an opinion of your first draft. She will explain that this is just a first draft, so, of course, it is not yet perfect. The editor will also be told that since you are the author, you have the right to take his/her advice or not. If your teacher decides, she might also place you in a cooperative learning support group.

Writer's Name_____

Editor's Name_____

PARTNER CHECKLIST

1. The original story had 22 sentences, minus the ending. How many sentences does this *recombined* and expanded version have?

2. Write the sentence number that is combined by:

    Glue words _____
    Connectors--**and, but, or** _____
    Colorful words in a series _____
    Verbs _____

3. Check to see that the author does not repeat the same sentence openings. If he does, which sentences would you recommend that he **combine** or **rearrange**?

4. If the author wrote a series of verbs or colorful words, did he punctuate correctly? If not, help him. Be a friend.

5. If the author circled words that he thinks are misspelled, check them to see if they are spelled correctly.

6. Are all the verbs in the present tense? They should be.

7. What do you like *best* about this rewritten paragraph?

8. How did the expanded ending add to your enjoyment of the story?

POLISHING UP YOUR FIRST DRAFT

Look at your **SOS**. Did you discover any places in your story that need changing? If so, go back to your draft and write in the changes. You are not required to complete a **Sentence Opening Sheet** for your final copy. Don't be worried about neatness as you rewrite the story. In fact, some writers call the changing of a draft *messification*.

Now look at the **Partner Checklist**. Did your editor discover any places that need improvement? If you agree with his opinion, go back to your draft and *messify* it.

STAGE FOUR: PUBLISHING

Since writing is for sharing ideas with other people, it is now time to un-messify your first draft and turn it into the Final Copy. Follow these tips to make a neat sheet:

- write neatly in ink with your best handwriting

- copy carefully including the changes

- no spelling circles--check the spelling

- no sentence numbers needed

Here's a fun idea for **Jan's Chance**. Why not create a baseball card? On the front of the card you can draw an illustration while on the backside you can include Jan's baseball statistics, such as batting average, home runs, teams played on, and a short biography. Use your imagination.

Oral Language into Writing

By this time you have probably realized that writing is not something anyone does *right* the first time. It is a means of trial and error. In fact, most professional writers spend almost as much time changing and re-working their sentences as they do writing the first draft.

Have you ever heard a popular song sung by two different groups? One band may sing it slower or throw in some different background music. Another might make the song seem sad and may use a female vocalist rather than a male vocalist. The fun comes in singing the same basic tune with different styles.

Writers can have the same kind of fun describing the same situation in different ways.

CREATING DIFFERENT MOODS FOR YOUR AUDIENCE

WARM-UP ACTIVITY 1

In this beginning oral activity, you and a partner can use your creative juices to try some different styles of writing. With your partner, describe each of the following situations as creatively as you can using no more than three sentences. This will be your first practice.

1. A little girl waiting for the bus on her first day of school

2. A woman waiting in the doorway of a small plane--just about ready to make a parachute jump

3. A surfer sitting on top of the board watching a huge wave approaching

4. A water skier going over a big jump in the middle of a lake

5. A basketball player who is slam-dunking the winning point of a game

6. A student waiting outside of the principal's office

Next, take the same situations and use completely different sentences to describe the same scene. You may want to change the **tone** the second time around to create a different mood or feeling for your audience.

For example, in your first set the scene might be happy and exciting. When you rewrite the same scene, you might want to make it frightening and scary.

There are all sorts of moods you could create, too. Make sure you have a completely different set of sentences. Write two sets of descriptions for three of the six situations.

Before you begin working with your partner, your teacher will model a situation with the entire class.

When the entire class is finished, you and your partner will have a chance to read your two versions aloud. Your classmates will vote to see which version best kept their interest.

Example:

A saleswoman who is working in a clothing department and sees a female customer.

TREATMENT ONE

The quivering saleslady was poised just to my right as I entered the door. Her eyes locked onto me like a heat-seeking missile, and instantly she darted through the racks and toward me. Blocking my progress and leaning into my face, she bleated anxiously, "Can I help you find anything?"

TREATMENT TWO

The store was sunny and calm with only a tinkling bell to announce my arrival. As I ambled through the wide aisles, I noticed a pleasant, grey-haired clerk humming to herself as she checked some figures. When I finally reached the back of the store, near her desk, she looked up, flashed a cheerful smile and said, "Hi. How are you on such a nice day?"

Be sure to share as many of the student examples as you can in an oral fashion.

Sentence Manipulation

COMBINING WITH WH WORDS

In the past units you practiced **combining** sentences with different structures. You will be interested to know that there are a few more tricks to learn when it comes to sentence **combining**. It's easy. To get started, check out the two sentences below:

> Sherry Simmons is shy. Sherry Simmons asked a question.

Here is a new way to *glue* two sentences together.

> Sherry Simmons, **who** is shy, asked a question.

You will notice that Sherry Simmons is used in both sentences. One *Sherry* is replaced by *who* to glue the sentences together. Here are some more sentences which are glued together in the same sort of way:

Examples:

1. I know the miserable man. The miserable man is my neighbor.

   I know the miserable man **who** is my neighbor.

2. Ben is six. Ben is one of my twin brothers.

   Ben, **who** is one of my twin brothers, is six.
   or
   Ben, **who** is six, is one of my twin brothers.

3. I like swimming. Swimming is my favorite summer sport.

   I like swimming **which** is my favorite summer sport.

4. Long John Silver's parrot was always on his shoulder. The parrot squawked, "Pieces of eight!"

   Long John Silver's parrot, **which** was always on his shoulder, squawked, "Pieces of eight!"

49

These words which connect sentences together are **WH words** because they begin with **WH**, except the word *that*. **WH words** are also called relative pronouns. Notice that **WH words** replace a repeated person, activity, or thing. They are placed right next to the word or words they replace. You must use **who**, **whose**, and **whom** for a human (or a pet): use **which** and **that** for a place, object, idea, action, or animal.

Here is a list of **WH words (relative pronouns)** and the words to which they refer:

who	people
whose	people
whom	people
which	things, objects, actions, ideas
that	places, objects, action, groups of people

Notice what can happen if the **WH word** (relative pronoun) is not placed next to the word it replaces.

Example:

Mimi was eating the octopus who is my sister.

Is Mimi or the octopus *my sister* according to this sentence? How would you correct this confusing sentence?

EXERCISE 1: Your turn now. Pick out the repeated word(s) and replace one of them with a **WH word** (relative pronoun) on a separate sheet of paper. Remember the **WH words** come right next to the word or words they replace. Do the first few as an oral activity.

Examples:

Cheryl served the buttered toast.
Cheryl works at Artie's Restaurant.

Cheryl, **who** served the buttered toast,
works at Artie's Restaurant.

NOT: Cheryl served the buttered toast, who works at Artie's Restaurant.

Cheryl works there, **not** the buttered toast.

1. Cheating is wrong.
   Cheating causes unfair grades.

2. The blazing fire started in the kitchen of the house.
   The blazing fire sent up black smoke.

3. Some odd people stood at my door.
   Some odd people were
   demonstrating vacuum cleaners.

4. Ruta's Restaurant serves the
   best sauerkraut soup.
   Ruta's Restaurant is my favorite
   place for lunch.

5. The old shoe is torn, scuffed,
   and tongueless.
   The old shoe belongs to Mrs. Hubbard.

6. Two alley cats screeched like badly played violins.
   Two alley cats fought all night.

7. Darin's pants are cutoff at the knees.
   Darin's pants keep his legs cool during the summer.

8. Your friend is playing the bugle.
   Henry George Michael Carmichael is your friend.

9. The invitation arrived three weeks before the party.
   The invitation smelled like roses.

10. Jogging is heavy exercise.
    Jogging sometimes causes injuries.

COMMA RULE 3

As you may have noticed, the **WH**-*clause*, which is located in the middle of the sentence, is set off by commas. Therefore, Comma Rule 3 reminds you to:

> Put a comma before and after the WH-clause if it comes in the middle of a combined sentence and is considered extra information.

This pattern for a combined sentence with a **WH-clause** looks like this:

My dog, which has fleas, is my best friend.
comma WH-clause   comma

In your punctuation rules notebook add Comma Rule 3. Also, write a sentence of your own which demonstrates this pattern of sentence punctuation.

HIDDEN WORDS

Sometimes the repeated word in the sentence is disguised or hidden by a pronoun, which is a word used to take the place of a noun.

Examples:

My cow gives chocolate milk. She is brown.

My cow, **which** gives chocolate milk, is brown.

As you can see, *my cow* is replaced by *she* in the second sentence. Nevertheless, both words stand for the same thing. Therefore, the sentences can be combined by using a **WH word** which can be substituted for any of them.

Person	Singular	Plural
First	I, me, my, mine	we, us, our, ours
Second	you, your, yours	you, your, yours
Third	he, him, his, hers	they, them, their
	it, its	theirs

EXERCISE 2: Modeling after the pattern sentence above, use the **WH words** *who, whose,* and *which* to combine these sentences. Each of these **WH words** must be used at least three times. Be sure to use commas where necessary.

1. Stanley stacks stones.
   He strolls to Steve's Sweet Shoppe.

2. Melissa and Martina modeled muu muus at Marshall's.
   They also marketed moccasins in Monterey.

3. James Harrington Chadwick speaks Swahili.
   He is chauffeur for Brigadier General Horace Honor.

4. Mt. Saint Helens volcano erupted on May 18, 1980.
   The eruption destroyed thousands of acres of forest.

5. My mother worked for a toy company.
   Her polka-dotted coat hung in the closet.

6. Delbert and Hector are graduating eighth-graders.
   They have the good luck to be going to
   Paul Robeson High School.

7. You are the newest salesman in the company.
   You led everyone else in sales this month.

8. I was given the unclaimed
fly swatter.
I had turned it into the office.

9. The troopers struggled in the
deep snow.
Their horses couldn't be ridden
much farther.

10. Our rent is due today.
If we can't pay it, we'll be evicted.

COMBINING WITH *WHOSE*

Some of the previous sentences have been easier to combine than others, haven't they? For instance, combining these two sentences with *whose* takes a little thinking.

Holly raises her own Percheron horses.
Her Buck and Billy won the horse pulls at the fair.

However, you can combine them just as you did the easier ones. Use *whose* to show ownership of something.

Holly, **whose** Buck and Billy won the horse pulls at the fair,
raises her own Percheron horses.

Here's another:

Matilda took second place in this year's roller derby.
Her sisters, Toby and Frances, won in past years.

Matilda, **whose** sisters Toby and Frances were winners in past
years, took second place in this year's roller derby.

Try a couple of these using *whose*.

1. Alena has a cat with no whiskers.
The cat looks like Tony the Tiger.

2. Toxico Chemical Co. was fined $2 million.
Its carelessness caused pollution.

COMBINING WITH *ING WORDS*

There is another trick to learn that can help you become an expert in sentence building. Again, to explain this trick, it's helpful to look at a way two sentences can be combined into one sentence.

      A. Daring Donald hurt his knee.
      B. Daring Donald jumped from the garage roof.

These two ideas can be combined like this:

      C. Daring Donald, jumping from the garage roof, hurt his knee.

As you noticed, *Daring Donald* is used in both sentences A and B. One *Daring Donald* is subtracted when *jumped* becomes *jumping* to glue the ideas together in the middle of the new combined sentence C.

When an **ING word** like *jumping* (a participle) is used, it begins a participial phrase. In addition, the same two sentences can be glued together with an **ING word** placed either at the beginning or near the end of the sentence.

Examples:

1 . Wendy was bored. She sat in the empty room.

    Sitting in the empty room, Wendy was bored.   (Sitting--beginning of sentence)
    Wendy was bored **sitting** in the empty room.   (Sitting--middle of sentence)

2 . My friend broke her tooth. She ate a rock.

    My friend broke her tooth **eating** a rock.   (Eating--end of sentence)
    Eating a rock, my friend broke her tooth.   (Eating--beginning of sentence)
    My friend, **eating** a rock, broke her tooth.   (Eating--middle of sentence)

3 . I watched the dull movie. I fell asleep.

    Watching the dull movie, I fell asleep.   (Watching--beginning of sentence)
    I fell asleep **watching** the dull movie.   (Watching--middle of sentence)

Now make two new sentences with your *Daring Donald* sentences A and B by first using an **ING word** at the beginning of one sentence, and then near the end of the other sentence.

You can make an **ING word** from almost any verb and use it as a sentence-combining word. Try. You'll see.

EXERCISE 3: Combine these sentences with **ING words**. You may use any of the three places which have been modeled. Combine each set in at least two different ways.

1. Lynne drives a sports car.
   Lynne easily out-drags everybody else.

2. Sheila looked for the boy.
   She found him in the trash can.

3. Carolyn feeds her guppies.
   She noticed that many of the little ones are missing.

4. We smiled nervously at Count Dracula.
   We wished we had not gone to his castle.

5. Sally jumped from the top of the jungle gym.
   Sally wore her Batgirl costume.

6. The baby smiled happily.
   She smeared glue in her hair.

7. The parakeet amuses Orville.
   The parakeet whistles *Dixie* in its cage.

8. The pig beats the heat.
   The pig snorts contentedly in the mud.

9. Beth opens the surprise package.
   She finds it contains only a rabbit's-foot key chain.

10. Mr. Tattan has become rich.
    He teaches spiders to make lace.

COMMA RULE 4

The ING word kernel (PARTICIPIAL PHRASE) which begins a combined sentence is followed by a comma.

Examples:

1. The house creaks at night.
   The house is spooky.

   Creaking at night, the house is spooky.

55

2. Karen was excited.
She packed for camp.
Packing for camp, Karen was excited.

3. Terry bought eighteen doughnuts.
Terry came home from work.
Coming home from work, Terry bought eighteen doughnuts.

4. Theresa pulled and tugged.
Theresa fixed the flat tire.
Pulling and **tugging**, Theresa fixed the flat tire.

Record this rule and your own model sentence in your punctuation rules notebook.

EXERCISE 4: Using **ING words**, combine the following sentences. Place your **ING word** at the beginning of the sentence. Make sure you correctly apply Rule 5. Before you start, pick out the action words (VERBS) in both sentences. Choose with care the one which you will change into an **ING word**.

1. The goalie blocked the shot.
She threw her hands into the air.

2. Aggie won the match point.
She smashed the serve out
of her opponent's reach.

3. Grace departed with
a tear in her eye.
She kissed her
mother good-bye.

4. Matthew Thomas ran
at full speed.
He tried to escape
from his brothers.

5. Lou raced towards home plate.
He attempted to break the tie game.

COMBINING AND CREATING A PARAGRAPH REVIEW

In a very short time you have learned to use **glue words**, **WH words**, and **ING words** to build sentences with many new looks. Let's see how creative you've become.

EXERCISE 5: To start, combine the small sentences in this paragraph into longer sentences using **glue words**, **WH words**, and **ING words**. Try to use each of the types of *glue* in at least one of the combined sentences you invent.

Before you begin combining, read the paragraph aloud two or three times to become familiar with its content.

The Mouse House

1. There is a hole. **2.** There is a wall. **3.** The hole is small. **4.** There is a kitchen.

5. A mouse runs. **6.** It is brown. **7.** It is tiny. **8.** It carries cheese. **9.** It has a mouth.

10. The mouse sees a cat. **11.** The mouse feels panic. **12.** The cat pounces. **13.** The mouse enters the hole. **14.** The mouse is happy. **15.** The mouse is safe. **16.** The cat moans. **17.** The cat feels sorry for itself. **18.** The cat is hungry.

EXERCISE 6: The next exercise is more challenging. As you read along, you see twenty-eight sentences which make up a short story. You are to combine the groups of sentences which have been divided into sections. Use the words listed at the top of each section as you combine the kernels in that section.

Even the Best Don't Win Every Time

Use **WH** and **ING words** for numbers 1-5 (two sentences)

1. Frosty Gill was a brain surgeon. **2.** He was muscular. **3.** He was lean. **4.** He stood over 6' 6" barefoot. **5.** He was an impressive looking man.

Use **glue words**, **because** and **although**, for 6-8

6. He wished to help the sick. **7.** He had studied medicine. **8.** He was an All-American basketball player.

Use **glue words, since** and **because**, for 9-12 (two sentences)

9. He was outstanding. **10.** He was offered several professional contracts. **11.** He was a helpful person. **12.** He became a brain surgeon in the end.

Use **glue word, whenever**, for 13-14

13. Frosty performed surgery. **14.** He worked with great care and prayerful concern for his patients.

Use **glue word, when**, for 15-16

15. The emergency room called him Monday night. **16.** He knew he would have to perform a miracle.

Use **glue word, while**, plus **ING word**, and **WH word, whose**, for 17-19

17. A little girl walked her dog. **18.** She had been struck by a hit-and-run driver. **19.** His car had no headlights.

Use **WH word** and **preposition, of** plus **ING word** for 20-21

20. The tiny patient was unconscious on the operating table. **21.** She had only a slim chance to survive her head injuries.

Use **ING word** for 22-23

22. Dr. Gill worked tirelessly over the child all night. **23.** He fought to save her life.

Use PREPOSITION, **in spite of**, and PREPOSITION, **without**, plus **ING word** for 24-26

24. His efforts were heroic. **25.** The little girl died. **26.** She did not regain consciousness.

Use **glue word, as**, for 27-28

27. Dr. Frosty Gill walked out of the hospital in the wet, grey dawn. **28.** He wished there was overtime in this life-and-death game.

So far in **Open the Deck** you have focused on the writing traits of word choice (**Unit 1**) and sentence fluency (**Unit 2**). Now your focus will be on organization--the order or sequence of your writing.

Good organization means that it is easy for your reader to follow from one idea to another. With good organization your ideas are organized into paragraphs with sentences that belong together. Poor organization means that the reader gets lost or confused by your writing.

In your next **Major Writing Assignment**, you will organize an Action Paper by writing with a beginning, a middle, and a climax at the end.

Plus, you will focus on the trait of **conventions**--mastery of the rules of writing. In this paper you must control verb tense so that all the verbs are in the past tense.

Helpful Drill Related to Word Choice

Read this action paper and see if you can follow the writer's ideas without getting lost. Is the organization easy to follow or is it confusing?

The Answer to a Maiden's Prayer

1. Hopping down the front steps after tossing the paper inside the hallway, Elsie sensed the growling presence of a dog. **2.** Tripping on her bulky paperbag. **3.** Elsie scrambles to her feet, seeking a place to hide. **4.** Showing his teeth, the dog stalks the frightened Elsie. **5.** With whimpering cries she plunged into the shrubs, cutting her hands on the barbed needles. **6.** Pursuing, the dog lunged into the shrubs after her.

7. Elsie cried for help, she picked herself up and ran toward the porch of a nearby house, praying like she was in church. **8.** The hairless Chihuahua easily overtakes her.

9. Instead of biting her, he began to wag his skinny, little tail. **10.** Elsie's prayers had been answered.

HELPFUL DRILL RELATED TO VERB TENSE

You undoubtedly already know this, but here's a quick reminder:

Present Tense	**Past Tense**
sprint/sprints	sprinted
slip/slips	slipped
run/runs	ran
swallow/swallows	swallowed
make/makes	made
build/builds	built

Now read the Action Paper again, this time hunting for two present tense verbs that should be in the past tense. Pro writers will find a third verb . . .

Major Writing Assignment

So far in *Open the Deck*, you have written papers describing a scene and **combining** and **expanding** sentences into a paragraph. In this assignment you get to practice another purpose: showing action and movement.

ING words, more than any other words in the English language, will help you show action and movement.

Here are examples of how **ING words** can be used to give the reader a sense of continuing movement.

Examples:

1. **Running down the stairs**, Kelsey bumped into Ms. Runnamaker.

2. **Skiing down the slope**, Diana felt that she owned the world.

As used above, the **ING words** are adjectives, aren't they? They describe someone.

3. **Biting** into a juicy hamburger relieved my hunger pains.

4. **Fixing** a flat tire can be tiresome.

As used in the preceding examples, the **ING words** are nouns. How are they different?

In addition, **ING words** can be used with present, past, and future verb tenses, too.

Examples:

1. Miguel **is yelling**.   Present Tense
2. Hampton **had been skipping**.   Past Tense
3. Quincy **will be singing**.   Future Tense

STAGE ONE: PREWRITING

STUDENT LEARNING OBJECTIVES

1. The student will describe a papergirl being chased by a dog.
2. The student will have solid organization, including a beginning, a middle, and an end to the story.
3. The student will use specific details and journalistic questions to make the story interesting.
4. The student will use **ING words** for action and movement.
5. The student will write all verbs in the past tense.

HELPFUL DRILL 1--ING WORDS TO THE RESCUE

Add **ING words** to complete these sentences.

Example: Moody Melissa was _____ comic books.
       Moody Melissa was **reading** comic books.

1. The flag was _____ in the wind.
2. Yan Ken was _____ over the hedges.
3. _____ through the mud, Willie crossed the goal line.
4. The ducks were _____ south for the winter.
5. _____ to the music made Lorenzo happy.
6. _____ a cow, old man MacDonald was kicked in the ribs.
7. Shirley is _____ in the shower.
8. The _____ wind tore the awnings from the building.
9. The frightened child, _____ in terror, ran from the haunted house.
10. _____ a bike tire can be tiresome.

HELPFUL DRILL 2--ING WORDS AS ADJECTIVES

Many times **ING words** are used as adjectives to describe a specific object or person. Look at the following examples.

1. the **creaking** house
2. my **aching** back
3. the **howling** werewolf
4. the **babbling** brook
5. the **wailing** siren

Add **ING** adjectives to describe the following nouns. After you add the **ING word**, expand the phrase with a past tense verb so that a sentence is formed. Complete this as a group activity.

62

Example:	Missing word	a _____wave
	Phrase	a **rolling** wave
	Sentence	A rolling wave **washed up** on the beach.

1. a_____brother
2. a_____bee
3. the_____car

4. a _____storm
5. a _____dancer

HELPFUL DRILL 3--SHOWING ACTION THROUGH VERBS

Change the past tense verb in one of these sentences to an **ING action word.**
Then combine the two sentences making one better sentence. Punctuate correctly.

Example: The halfback **ran** down the field.
            He **scored** a touchdown.

            Running down the field, the halfback scored a touchdown.

                          or

            The halfback, **scoring** a touchdown, ran down the field.

1. The old-fashioned radiator leaked.
   The radiator flooded the basement.

2. The policewoman drove through the alley.
   She noticed an open window.

3. Nick raced through the hallway.
   He tripped over a pencil.

4. The hamburger sizzled on the grill.
   It looked mouth-watering.

5. The eagle soared high in the heavens.
   The eagle peered down on the tiny mouse.

6. The tractors rumbled down the highway.
   The tractors caused a traffic jam.

7. The tooth fairy quietly tiptoed into my room.
   She left a dollar under my pillow.

8. Sammy arrived early for the surprise party.
   Sammy helped Carmen decorate the basement.

WRITING PROMPT

Looking out your living room window, you see your papergirl, Elsie Truhart, being chased by a dog. To practice using **ING words** to describe a situation, you will write a descriptive paragraph starting with this opening sentence.

> **Hopping** down the front steps after **tossing** the paper inside
> the hallway, Elsie sensed the **growling** presence of a dog.

ORGANIZING YOUR IDEAS

Beginning with Elsie's hearing the dog until the end of the scene, organize your ideas in a time sequence. You will be scored on your ability to do this trait.

Write what happens from the beginning to the end. **Expand** with as many specific details as possible to make the story more interesting. Stretch! Use the journalistic questions if you are having difficulty thinking of specific details. Whether the story has a sad or happy ending is up to you.

Consider using some of the following **ING action words** or any of your own:

1. screaming	10. dodging	19. attacking	28. licking
2. yelling	11. petting	20. praying	29. whistling
3. jumping	12. frowning	21. snarling	30. hearing
4. tripping	13. surrendering	22. wagging	31. careening
5. falling	14. fleeing	23. smiling	32. crawling
6. crying	15. whimpering	24. growling	33. training
7. barking	16. slipping	25. feeding	34. laughing
8. lunging	17. tearing	26. springing	35. petting
9. maneuvering	18. ripping	27. pawing	36. thanking

Also consider using some of the following objects for your scene:

1. paperbag	10. mailbox	19. porch	28. steps
2. clothesline	11. alley	20. bike	29. net
3. railing	12. open garage	21. grocery store	30. birdbath
4. fence	13. doghouse	22. hydrant	31. treehouse
5. lawn	14. garbage cans	23. rake	32. tomcat
6. shrubs	15. manhole	24. telephone pole	33. church
7. trees	16. swimming hole	25. hedges	34. cars
8. gutter	17. church steeple	26. driveway	35. sewer
9. water hose	18. motorcycle	27. gangway	36. luggage

GLUING IDEAS TOGETHER

In this action paper both Elsie and the dog will be in *motion*. Sometimes Elsie may move and the dog will follow. Sometimes the dog may make a move, then Elsie. Use some of the following glue words and transition words as you move from sentence to sentence. This will help your reader follow your story's sequence.

Here are two lists of words that can be used to connect ideas:

after	now
until	finally
as	then
before	during
while	once
when	at last

In using these words to **combine** sentences, you must be careful that you do not confuse your audience. You must state exactly what you want to say. As a group project, discuss the different meanings with these sentences.

A. Since the mouse was restless, he paced back and forth.

B. Since the mouse paced back and forth, he was restless.

What's the difference in meaning between these two sentences?

THINK SHEET

Before you begin to write your first draft, you need to fill out the special **Think Sheet**. Jot down specific, imaginative ideas. List one event after the other.

With each event, expand with specific details to make your story more interesting. Remember, you can always add to or subtract from your list once you begin to write your paper.

ACTION PAPER THINK SHEET

Purpose: You will describe Elsie's dangerous situation, using **ING action words**.

1 . The scene-setter and action-starter sentence, given to you earlier, is your launching device for this composition.

> Hopping down the front steps after tossing the paper inside the hallway, Elsie sensed the growling presence of a dog.

2 . List in sequence what happened afterwards. The action you describe must include a beginning, a middle, and an ending. To all actions, **expand** with specific details to make them clearer to your reader. Use a separate piece of paper so that you can be sure to record enough information under each category.

Elsie's Actions	**Specific Details**	**Dog's Actions**
1. The beginning action		
2. The middle actions		
3.		
4.		
5.		
6.		
7.		
8. The climax!		

3.   What type of ending will Elsie experience? Describe it.

STAGE TWO: WRITING THE FIRST DRAFT

When you have completed your **Think Sheet** and planned your paper, you may begin to write your first draft. Follow the same drafting tips as before.

SENTENCE OPENING SHEET

Be sure to fill out a **Sentence Opening Sheet** supplied by your teacher after you have completed the first draft. Remember that you will need to number each of your sentences.

Check your completed **Sentence Opening Sheet** for the following points:

1. Variety in sentence openings. Some of your sentences should begin with **ING** phrases. Remember how to punctuate them. (Column 1)
2. Include all **ING words** in the special column (Column 2). This will tell you how many **ING words** you have included.
3. Make sure all of your verbs are in the past tense. Check your verb column for this. (Column 3)
4. Check to see if you repeat the same verbs over and over again, or if you have a variety. (Column 3)
5. If your sentences are too short and choppy, you may want to combine some of them. (Column 4)

STAGE THREE: REWRITING

You might have to review some rules before you critique the student model on page 59, **The Answer to a Maiden's Prayer**. You might also want to use the grading sheet--scoring rubric-- your teacher distributed in the prewriting stage.

Before you exchange papers with your proofreading partner(s), read the student's first draft and answer the following questions.

1. In which sentences did the writer use present tense verbs instead of past tense?
2. In which sentence does a run-on occur?
3. In which ways can the writer make this story more interesting?
4. Identify the fragment. Correct it by combining it with another sentence.

Now exchange first drafts with your partner or team. Use the following **Checklist Sheet** as your guide. Write your answers on a separate piece of paper. If you want, refer to sentences by number.

Also, don't be afraid to make suggestions on the author's paper, but remember that the author makes the final decisions. He *owns* the paper.

AN ACTION WORD PAPER CHECKLIST

1. How many **ING action words** did the writer use? If you feel the story needs more **ING action words**, suggest them on the writer's draft in the margin.

2. If the writer began any sentences with **ING action words**, are they punctuated correctly? If not, help him? Be a friend.

3. All the verbs should be in the past tense. If any are in the present tense, correct them on the first draft.

4. What other actions could the writer have included to make the paper more interesting? Indicate this on the first draft.

5. What is the one thing the writer could have done to improve the story?

6. What do you like best about this paper?

STAGE FOUR: PUBLISHING

Your teacher may choose to read several final papers aloud to the class. As a group you can discuss how each paper best conveyed the action of poor Elsie's dilemma.

If you are a Michangelo, you might want to illustrate Elsie's dilemma with an award-winning drawing. These classic pieces of art could be hung in your classroom.

Oral Language into Writing

In **Unit 1** you *discovered* that words can be used as both nouns and verbs. This time you are going one step further by creating verbs out of familiar nouns. This is called coining words. Not only is this fun, but it will also help you increase your vocabulary, making your sentences come alive.

You are connecting oral language with written language.

NEVER HEARD BEFORE VERBS

WARM-UP ACTIVITY 1

In the following sentences notice the coined verbs. Discuss the meanings of the **bold** verbs.

1. Grandma **lightbulbs** her new lamp.
2. The cat **defished** my plate.
3. For a late night snack, Uncle Wally **turkeyed** the bread.
4. Dad **pillowed** the guest room bed.
5. Before the storm, Mom **garaged** the car.
6. I **will mustard** my hot dog before adding hot peppers.
7. Wendell **basemented** the old kitchen chairs.
8. Juanita **arrowed** her bow as the wolves approached.
9. Stacey **bucketed** the ball from fifteen feet.
10. Kira **forked** the big potato.
11. Adam, the teacher's pet, **appled** Miss Child's desk.
12. Uncle Albie **bearded** his face.
13. Norma **nickled** the parking meter.
14. Jack **beanstalked** to the giant's house.
15. Felipe **grandslammed** the winning runs.
16. Liz **gloved** the fly ball.
17. Sarasta **penciled in** the missing answer.
18. Because Yolanda spilled the hot chocolate on her new dress, she **soaped** the spotted area immediately.
19. Yum Kin **was sandwiched** between two heavyweight wrestlers on his flight from Hong Kong.
20. Harry **sardined** his peanut butter and jelly sandwich.

ADDING VERBS TO OUR LANGUAGE

Verbs are constantly being added to our language. In fact, whenever a new noun (thing word) was added, its verb usually follows.

Examples:

Nouns	Verbs
1. Marcia orders a **telephone**.	1. Marcia **telephoned** home.
2. Kyle has a **vacuum cleaner**.	2. Kyle **vacuumed** her rug.
3. Lionel poured some **salt**.	3. Lionel **salted** his eggs.
4. Jacinda used a **fax** machine.	4. Jacinda **faxed** her order.
5. Hoppie owns a **saddle**.	5. Hoppie **saddled** his pony.

Not all *things* have a matching verb, though. At least not yet. You can *coin* (make-up) verbs for these things.

WARM-UP ACTIVITY 2

On a separate sheet, *paper* new verbs for the following nouns. In other words, write a new verb for each noun. Then use them in sentences.

Examples:

	noun	verb	sentence
a.	cat	catted	The Millers *catted* their cellar to solve the mice problem.
b.	strawberry	strawberried	Aunt Josie *strawberried* the pie.
c.	ace	aced	Kenya *aced* her math test.

1. glove	7. blackboard	13. fireplace
2. garbage	8. tomato	14. tuna
3. handrail	9. deck	15. roof
4. shirt	10. paper	16. blister
5. lawn	11. can	17. your choice
6. balloon	12. sky	18. your choice

WARM-UP ACTIVITY 3

Use your imagination and write a story using some of the creative verbs you have coined. Originality counts.

COMBINING SENTENCES WITH VERBS

In **Unit 1** you **combined** sentences with colorful words. Here is another way to **combine** sentences. Look at the sentences below:

> Abe cleaned his room.
> Abe dusted his computer.

As you can see, Abe is the Doer (subject) in both sentences. Only the action changes. It is possible to make a new, **expanded** sentence which ties in both verbs.

> Abe **cleaned** his room and **dusted** his computer.

In the sentence above, **and**, a connector or conjunction, was used to tie together both verbs.

Sometimes a writer may want to include more than two verbs in one sentence. Look at this example.

> The runner took off her sweats, tied her running shoes,
> **and** warmed-up for the six mile jog.

In this type of sentence, three verbs have been tied together. Look at the sentence again. Notice that the writer used two commas and one connector to make the new sentence. The commas and connector are in **bold**.

EXERCISE 1: See if you can **combine** the following sets of sentences into one sentence which includes more than two verbs. Pay close attention to the two sentence combining examples you've just been given. Note that the two-verb model does not need a comma. However, the three-verb model does. Use the same patterns in the sentences you write. Complete the first one as a class activity.

1. Minnie made mud pies.
   Minnie baked them carefully.
   Minnie gobbled them down.

2. The actress painted her wrinkled skin.
   The actress glued on false eyelashes.
   The actress plopped on a bright, red wig.

3. The puppet came to life.
   The puppet danced with the teddy bears.
   The puppet then went back to sleep.

4 . The pinch hitter bounced a single to center.
The pinch hitter slid into second base.
The pinch hitter swallowed a pound of dust.

5 . We made our beds.
We hung up our clothes.
We hated every minute of it.

COMBINING WITH *AND, BUT,* AND *OR*

Sometimes the simplest way to expand a sentence is to **combine** it with another complete sentence. In order to do this, **combine** using one of these connectors (conjunctions):

and	=	joins names, things, actions, and ideas
but	=	shows a difference
or	=	offers a choice

Look at these two separate sentences.

1 . Fernando passes the basketball to the big man.
2 . The quick defense player knocks it out of bounds.

How can you combine these two separate sentences with the connector (conjunction) **but** to create a better sentence?

Fernando passes the ball to the big man, **but**
the quick defense player knocks it out of bounds.

EXERCISE 2: Now it's your turn to combine these sentence sets in the same way. Remember to insert a comma right before the connector (conjunction) **and, but,** and **or**. Do the first one as a group activity.

1 . My little brother, Davey, made my bed for me.
I wondered if he had short-sheeted it.

2 . I wanted to paint my room red and black.
My Mom looked sick and said, "No!"

3 . Hector could walk to the movie.
He could sit at home and sulk.

4 . Professor Sagorsky had picked the
Lotto Jackpot numbers.
He threw away the winning ticket by mistake.

5 . With my graduation gift I can buy a CD player.
I can donate the money to the homeless.

COMMA RULE 5

In these exercises, you have been using a comma right before each connector (conjunction). This is the fifth comma rule which you should record in your punctuation rules notebook.

> When two complete ideas are joined together with a connector such as **and**, **but**, or **or**, a comma must be placed right *before* the connector (conjunction).

These examples, plus your own, model this rule.

1. My brother played a good game, **but** I finally beat him.
2. The woodpecker drove Horace crazy, **and** he finally bought earplugs.

Now try your hand at writing sentences by modeling the above examples and expanding with your own information. Follow the guide words below.

DOER	DID	, AND	DOER	DID

6. _____

7. _____ , **but**_____

8. _____ , **or**_____

EXERCISE 3: Continue on and combine the following sentences.

1. Arief must cut the lawn.
   He will not receive his allowance.

2. I tried to change Sylvester's mind.
   It was a hopeless attempt.

3. The fleas in my bedroom are big and hungry.
   They don't make my bed either.

4. The tractor rolled over the muddy ground.
   The cows looked unconcerned as the contraption approached.

5. My homework isn't finished.
   My favorite program starts in five minutes.

WRITING WARM-UP

USING YOUR WRITER'S VOCABULARY TO COMPOSE

EXERCISE 4: Complete this next activity as a class project. Rewrite the paragraph and combine the pairs which are presented in each numbered set. Each of the connectors--**and, but, or**--must be used twice in **Swamp Madness**. Before you begin to combine, read the story aloud as one paragraph.

Swamp Madness

1. The night was evil.
2. The man in the moon had an innocent smile on his face.

3. Gentle waves lapped at the rocks.
4. Water lilies decorated the shallows of the lake.

5. The lovely lake seemed peaceful enough.
6. Beneath the murky waters lurked the creature.

7. The villagers knew they should avoid the lake after nightfall.
8. They would become the prey of the creature.

9. Tonight it was hungry.
10. Tonight it was searching the shoreline for food.

11. The victim must be found before daybreak.
12. The creature would go hungry.

After you have created the new paragraph, read it aloud to hear the differences from the original model.

CONNECTING THE SKILLS

EXERCISE 5: Finally, it's time for you to work completely on your own. On the next page are groups of sentences. See if you can combine the grouped sentences, using any of the sentence combining techniques--**writer's vocabulary**--you have learned so far in *Open the Deck*.

Here's a quick review:

- expand on some information by asking **who, what, when, where, why** and **how** journalistic questions
- coining some new words--verbs
- using verbs to combine related ideas
- combining with connectors--**and, but, or**--to link two complete sentences

Write your new sentences in paragraph form. Your most important job, however, is to try to **expand**. Stretch some of your sentences to make them more interesting for your audience. Tell not only what happens, but also explain in detail how it happens.

Invent an original conclusion for **Ditched**. Use your imagination. Get your creative juices flowing.

Ditched!

1. I was heading home in my beat-up car.
2. The night was pitch black.

3. The rain was coming down hard.
4. The window on my side of the car was broken.

5. My wipers worked hard to clear my windshield.
6. I had trouble seeing the road.

7. I could pull off to the side of the road.
8. I could try to continue home through the storm.

9. I saw dim headlights coming towards me
10. The lights were on my side of the road.

11. Maybe the driver of the oncoming car was panicked.
12. Maybe he didn't see my low beams.
13. That was it.

14. I flicked my headlights as a warning.
15. The oncoming car didn't change lanes.

16. I could try to play dodgem with him on the slippery road.
17. I could put my old beater in the ditch.

18. I cut the steering wheel hard to the right.

19. I landed upside down in the irrigation ditch.
20. Water rushed in through the broken window.

MAJOR WRITING ASSIGNMENT

Persuading

STAGE ONE: PREWRITING

So far in *Open the Deck* you have had a chance to practice some sentence **combining** skills and a few comma rules. Mastering these writing strategies is important because you need to use them in everyday writing projects of your own. People of all ages use writing to help present their own ideas in a convincing way.

Persuading somebody else of your viewpoint is a strength which is very important in any classroom and later on in your career. Many times this kind of persuasion occurs in a letter format--often a business letter.

You probably realize that not all letters are friendly letters written to deliver a personal message. Often it is necessary to send a businesslike message to a store or company. The message can be to place or cancel an order, to ask for information, to complain, to praise, or to request that the company do something for you.

Also, the tone or sound of a business letter is more formal than that of a friendly letter.

In this unit you will be writing a business letter to a company complaining either about a product you purchased or about an inadequate service you received.

STUDENT LEARNING OBJECTIVES

1. The student will write a business letter to a company.
2. The student's letter will include the six parts of a business letter: the heading, the inside address, the greeting, the body, the closing, and the signature.
3. The student will include specific information in the body of the letter, including reasons to support the request.
4. The student will write with a strong voice.
5. The student will punctuate the greeting, addresses, and closing correctly.
6. The student will address an envelope correctly.
7. The student will apply simple sentence combining ideas.
8. The student will capitalize the correct words.

Focused Writing Traits

Good writers are those who have mastered the traits of quality writing. Traits are characteristics, the qualities, of someone or something. For example, here are some traits of a quality birthday party; you may be able to add a few more:

- plenty of food
- good music
- games to play
- lots of noise
- birthday cake (with seconds and thirds)
-
-

Now, in this major writing assignment, the persuasive business letter, you will focus on two traits:

- voice: the true sound of you coming through the writing
- ideas: powerful reasons to support your opinion

Voice means that you put honest feelings into your written words. The reader of your business letter can easily tell that you really care about this topic. Your purpose rings true and clear. However, you need to be careful and not over-do it.

Remember your purpose is to convince someone that you are right, and you deserve something to be done for you. So do not use an angry, snide, or threatening tone of voice--which very likely would turn off your reader and prevent you from successful persuading.

Ideas means the quality of what you are writing about. Strong ideas make for clear, focused, and interesting writing that holds your reader's attention to your letter. Because your purpose is to persuade, to convince the reader, your ideas must include strong reasons to support your opinion of what should happen.

Remember this: the stronger the reasons, the better your chance for getting your way.

BUSINESS LETTER FORMAT

Unlike the friendly letter, the business letter consists of six parts: the heading, inside address, greeting, body, closing, and signature.

There are two basic styles: the full-block and the semi-block. The placement of the six parts is somewhat different in each style.

1. The **heading** includes your street address, city, state, zip, and date.
2. The **inside address** includes the name and complete address of the person and/or company receiving the letter.
3. The **greeting** opens the letter and ends with a colon(:) instead of a comma. For a specific person, use a greeting like *Dear Mrs. ( ):* For a company or organization, use *Gentlemen:, Dear Sirs:,* or *Dear Sir or Madam:.*
4. The **body** contains the message. Since business people are busy, your letter should be concise. Use little or no flowery language.
5. The **closing** is spaced two spaces below the body. Use *Yours truly,* or *Sincerely,* for the closing. Place a comma at the end of the closing.
6. Your full **signature** should end the letter.

Here are two examples of the full-block and semi-block letter formats.

Full-Block / Semi-Block

WRITING INSIDE ADDRESSES AND GREETINGS

EXERCISE 6: Write the inside address for a business letter to these companies, using the following information.

1. Consumer Department Manager, Quill Paper Co., 109 W. Shriek Alley, Brainy Boro, New Jersey 08840

2. John B. Cufflink, Lucky Charms, Inc., 200 N. Wishbone Blvd., Luckey, Ohio 43443

3. Loan Department, Federal Reserve Bank, 30 Pearl Street, Boston, Massachusetts 02110

4. Desk Clerk, Edge-O-Town Motel, 2 Weaverville Highway, Asheville, North Carolina 28804

5. Alice Gust, Gusty Windmill Company, 3321 Breeze Way, Cyclone, Pennsylvania 16726

6. Saskatoon Metal, 3456 Flatbed Road, Saskatoon, Saskatchewan L3X 6P2

7. Big Horn Realty, 4534 South Skyline Boulevard, Cheyenne, Wyoming 82036

8. Happy Home Shopper, P. O. Box 4730, Lubbock, Texas 79438

9. California Bell, 2020 Circuit Breaker Road, West Hollywood, California 90690

10. R Place Hideaway, 9682 Welsch Road, Winnecone, Wisconsin 54986

EXERCISE 7: Write a business letter greeting to these people, punctuating properly.

1. Ms. Donna Ogle
2. Dr. Josephine DePino
3. Mr. Othel Preswick
4. Wally Potts
5. To a person with an unknown name

EVALUATING BUSINESS LETTERS

Have you ever been disappointed after buying something that didn't quite work out as you expected? Maybe you bought a pair of jeans that frayed at the seams after only a few months. Maybe you joined a record/tape/CD club through the mail, but you didn't get what you thought you had ordered. Or have you ever been treated unfairly because *you're just a kid*?

In this unit you will learn how to write a business letter of complaint in order to get your money back, obtain an exchange, or express your feelings about some poor treatment you received.

Suppose you saw an ad in a comic book or magazine about plastic insects that look so real that they are guaranteed to scare anybody. Of course, you ordered some by sending in the order form, along with a check for $4.98.

After waiting six weeks, you finally received a package of the creepy crawlers. Unfortunately, the plastic bugs were not real looking. In fact, they didn't fool your three-year-old brother, your grandmother, or even Mikey the kid next door, who falls for anything. Since The Creepy Crawler Company guaranteed the bugs to be scary, you want your money back.

The purpose of your letter, then, is to write The Creepy Crawler Company and ask for a refund of your money.

On the next page are two letters written by Wayne Fontana. Decide which letter Wayne should mail to The Creepy Crawler Company before you write your letter of complaint.

Successful letters of complaint have five key parts:

- Where and when you bought the product.
- How much you paid for it.
- Why you are dissatisfied with it--what's wrong with it? Remember to give reasons--trait 1.
- What do you want the company to do?
- The voice (sound or tone) of the letter is important--trait 2.

Discuss with your class these five key parts for both letters. Which letter has the best chance for success? Also, help Wayne out by removing any errors in spelling, punctuation, and capitalization.

2145 Lincoln
Eugene, Oregon 97405
May 20, 1999

Customer Relations
Creepy Crawler Company
3044 Spiderlegs Ave. NW
Garfield Heights, Ohio 44123

Dear Sir or Madam:

What a giant rip-off!!!! Your stupid
plastic bugs didn't even scare Mikey
next door. You can have them back,
and I want my money back.

Sincerely,

**Wayne's Letter
Written in Full-
Block Format
(LEFT)**

**Wayne's Letter
Written in
Semi-Block Format
(BELOW)**

2145 Lincoln
Eugene, OR 97405
May 20, 1999

Customer Relations
The Creepy Crawler Company
3044 Spiderlegs Avenue NW
Garfield Heights, Ohio 44123

Gentlemen:

After reading your ad for creepy crawlers in *Slime*
magazine, I could hardly wait to own a set. I anticipated
pranking the entire neighborhood with the bugs you
guaranteed to be scary. Unfortunately, they were a
tremendous disappointment. They didn't even fool
Mikey, the little kid next door.

Enclosed you will find the creepy crawlers I received.
Please back up your guarantee by promptly refunding
my money in the amount of $4.98. Thank you.

Sincerely,

WRITING PROMPT

Now it's your turn to write a business letter following the format we just described.

Before you begin to write your own letter of complaint, fill out the following **Think Sheet**. It will give you plenty of ideas to include on your first draft.

It is much better to select a subject from which you have had personal dealings. Maybe you weren't satisfied with a specific product you bought? Maybe you were treated *unfairly* or discourteously by a salesperson or clerk in your favorite store or fast food restaurant?

As a group activity, you might want to brainstorm about products or services in which you have had some problems. Your story might trigger a memory in a classmate.

BUSINESS LETTER THINK SHEET

Purpose: You will write a business letter to a company, asking either for a refund for a product or specific satisfaction from discourteous service.

1. What store were you in?

2. When were you in there (date, time)?

3. What product did you buy or what service are you complaining about?

4. What was wrong with the product or service?

5. Why are you writing the company? What is your purpose? What do you want the company to do?

6. What tone of voice (trait 1) do you think will be best to achieve your purpose? Will you sound angry, sad, polite, threatening, pleasant, firm, pleading, funny? Why?

7. What reasons (trait 2) do you have to support your request? Present at least two. **Expand** all of the reasons to make them convincing and persuasive.

8. Under what conditions will you propose to return the faulty product and receive your refund?

9. Using your address and today's date, write the heading for your letter.

10. Write an inside address for the company. If you have a real product, find the real company's address. If you are inventing a product, make up an address.

11. With what greeting will you begin your letter? What punctuation mark comes at the end of the greeting?

12. What closing will you use?   Sincerely,   From,   Your friend,
                                       Yours truly,

STAGE TWO: WRITING THE FIRST DRAFT

Once your **Think Sheet** is completed, write your first draft. Use the **Think Sheet** as your map, but feel free to change some ideas as you write.

Here are some points to remember as you draft:

- Include all the major parts of a business letter.

- Try to write at least two sentences which use connecting words or items in a series.

- Be sure to follow the drafting rules you learned in **Unit 1**, page 20.

STAGE THREE: REWRITING

This third stage of the writing process is very important. It is also the most difficult stage because now it's time to switch from the *quickly getting your ideas down on paper* of the drafting stage to the *slowly checking over the paper* of the rewriting stage.

Before rewriting your final copy, you will once again exchange papers with your proofreading partner or support group. You will use the **Checklist Sheet** on the next page as your guide so that you are checking your partner's paper for very specific points. You might also use the grading sheet (rubric) your teacher distributed during the prewriting stage.

Your teacher may also put you in cooperative learning groups. One individual in the group may be responsible for numbers 1-4; the second person, 5-7; the third person, 8-10.

Treat your partner's paper as if it were your own.

Remember: you are giving friendly, helpful advice.

Be supportive and positive while being honest.

BUSINESS LETTER CHECKLIST

1. What is the writer's purpose?

2. What is the tone of voice? How does it sound to you?

   a. polite **b.** angry   **c.** funny   **d.** unsure   **e.** firm
   f. other____

3. What reasons are given to support the writer's request?

4. If you were the person receiving the letter, possibly the Consumer Service Manager, would you agree with the writer and refund the money or honor the request? Why or why not?

5. Check the organization of the letter. Are its six parts correctly placed?

6. What sentences used connector words?

7. Do you find any capital letter errors or punctuation errors?

8. Does a colon (:) come after the greeting? Is the closing punctuated correctly?

9. If the writer used the semi-block format, did she/he indent each paragraph?

10. What is your favorite part of the letter?

REVISING YOUR FIRST DRAFT

Now that your partner has given you some advice on the **Checklist Sheet**, you have some decisions to make. Are there any changes you want to make in your letter? What is suggested? Do you agree?

Here are some items you might consider in rewriting your first draft:

1. add some new information
2. cross out or erase sentences you no longer need
3. change some words to be more specific
4. add some capital letters
5. put in a colon after the greeting
6. move parts around to make the organization better
7. cross out misspelled words and replace them with correct spellings
8. rearrange some sentences for variety
9. indent paragraphs in the semi-block format
10. other--your choice

At the top of your draft write the number of at least one change you will make. Now find the place in your draft and make the changes. This is called *messification*. Don't be shy--get to it!

STAGE FOUR: PUBLISHING

A FRESH COPY

Of course, you now must *unmessify* your letter. Recopy it neatly onto a fresh sheet of paper including any changes you made.

> Write in ink.
> Best handwriting.
> Spell correctly.
> Be neat.
> Do not skip lines.
> Do not number the sentences.

Your teacher will give you an envelope to address to the company. Be sure to properly address it by writing your return address in the upper left corner and the company's address in the center of the envelope.

Wayne   Fontana
2145 Lincoln
Eugene, OR 97405

Customer Relations
The Creepy Crawler Company
3044 Spiderlegs Avenue NW
Garfield Heights, OH 44123

MAIL CALL

Mail the letter to the company if you have written about a real product. Don't forget the stamp.

Oral Language into Writing

MANY MEANINGS OF A WORD

Words can have many meanings. For example, if you were asked to tell what the word *curb* means, you would probably say something like, *the raised edge of the street*. But if the word *curb* is used in the sentence which follows, it has another meaning.

Mom chews gum to **curb** her desire to smoke cigarettes.

Of course, Mom is not sitting on the raised edge of the street, trying to give up smoking. *Curb* in this new sentence means *to hold back* or *to reduce*. *Curb* can be both a noun (a cement thing on the side of the street) and a verb (to hold back).

WARM-UP ACTIVITY 1

Let's play around with a few words doing double duty. On a separate sheet of paper, write down what you believe to be the meaning of each of the following words. Then, read the matching sentences below to see if that meaning makes sense.

1. hound
2. sling
3. cave

4. hard
5. seal

1. Little Wilbur will hound the family's hound until the dog agrees to play with him.
2. Because his arm was in a sling, David could not sling a stone at Goliath.
3. The bright sunshine caused our snow cave to cave in.
4. Hard-headed Hugh is hard of hearing, but tries hard to listen.
5. Albert forgot to seal the seal's cage.

WARM-UP ACTIVITY 2

Work with a partner or your cooperative learning group and complete this warm-up activity. On a separate sheet of paper, write one sentence using two meanings for the following words:

		1 2
Example:	**suit**	Does my **suit suit** you?

meaning 1	a garment; clothes
meaning 2	appeal to you

1. cup	**4.** soil
2. duck	**5.** bore
3. light	

STRETCHED MEANINGS--IDIOMS

Not only do many of our language's words have several meanings, but they are also used in an informal way--slang. These stretched meanings are called idioms.

WARM-UP ACTIVITY 3

Tell how the meanings of the following words were stretched in these idioms.

1.	hair	It was a *hairy* problem.
2.	lost	Mr. Murray told me to *get lost*.
3.	hand	The teacher gave the students a *handout*.
4.	leaf	I'm going to *turn over a new leaf* and faithfully do my chores.
5.	snake	We don't trust him because he's a *snake in the grass*.
6.	glass	The boxer retired from the ring since he had a *glass jaw*.
7.	horses	*Hold your horses*.
8.	monkey	Quit *monkeying around* and get to work!
9.	fishtail	The speeding car *fishtailed* along the icy road.
10.	bug	That crazy song really *bugs* me.

Make up a list of five of your own word stretches--idioms. Ask your parents, grandparents, Uncle Harvey, or friends for help. Share your final list with the rest of the class. See if they can figure out the meanings. Why not publish a list of idioms, illustrating each of them with a creative drawing?

WARM-UP ACTIVITY 4

Study the many meanings of the word *glass* from the sixth sentence in the previous activity.

6. glass   The boxer retired from the ring since he had a *glass jaw*.

    a. a glassy-eyed person
    b. ice as smooth as glass
    c. a looking glass
    d. a glass house
    e. drink from a glass

Now see if you can come up with five different meanings for the word *hand* in the third sentence. Write your examples on a sheet of paper and share them orally with the class. You might also want to complete this as a cooperative learning activity.

TOM SWIFTIES

WARM-UP ACTIVITY 5

Another way that people have had fun with language is to come up with adverbs which have a catchy connection to the action of the sentence.

Here are some examples:

1. "I can't wait to eat all those bon bons," she said *sweetly*.
2. "Don't cut yourself on the knives," the mother said *sharply*.
3. "This hill was a little more steep than I thought," the mountain climber said *puffily*.
4. "What's the deal with my nose?" Pinocchio said *pointedly*.
5. "I think you put a little too much starch in my collar," Dad said *stiffly*.

These types of language stretches are also called **TOM SWIFTIES**.

Working with a partner, try to come up with four or five swifties of your own. These can be shared with the entire class. See which examples cause the most groans.

Sentence Manipulation

So far in *Open the Deck* you have practiced **combining** and **expanding** sentences--your **writer's vocabulary words**. Usually this practice results in better sentences and more variety in sentence openings and structures.

Sometimes, however, a writer will intend to combine sentences but will forget to write them as a completed sentence. These lonesome pieces are called fragments, or FRAGS, for short. They can be a very big problem for many young writers.

FRAGMENT TIP NUMBER 1

Fragments often begin with words that we have already studied: **glue words**, **WH words**, and **ING words**.

Example: Robin was surprised. **Because** the mouse roared.

The writer of these two clauses thought about combining them using the **glue word** *because*. However, these clauses weren't written that way. The clause that begins with *because* was left all by itself. It is lonesome. It is called a fragment.

EXERCISE 1: Look at more examples of lonesome fragments. Pick out the **glue words**, **WH words**, and **ING words** that begin the fragments.

1. The Blue Jays travel to Seattle next week. Starting their first road trip of the season.
2. Maisie moistens Mom's famous pie dough. Which is the secret step in the recipe.
3. Dad and Uncle Chester dragged the ladder to the porch. In order to rescue the family's porcupine.
4. Forgetful Foster parks his juicy wad of chewing gum. Because it was old.
5. Steady Eddie Stanwick, the star state trooper, speeds to the scene of the crime. Leaving his ticket book back at Pancho's Diner.
6. A nervous caterpillar waited inside the mailbox. Until someone opened the door.
7. Jumping Joe Johnson jams the basketball. While the crowd goes wild.
8. Our town's mayor and her husband are visiting relatives in Montreal. Until the holidays are over.
9. Jerome and Jessie have been doing handstands for ten minutes. Waiting for Ms. Wilkie to open the gym.
10. Several space travelers landed in Ms. Hooper's flower garden. Even though they were aiming for the swimming pool.

FRAGMENT TIP NUMBER 2

If you had a difficult time hearing fragments in the previous practice, we have a special tip for you.

Why not try reading your paper backwards-- in reverse order-- one sentence at a time? Begin with the last sentence and stop. See if it makes sense. Let's try one from the previous activity:

> The Blue Jays travel to Seattle next week. Starting their
> first road trip of the season.

Read the last sentence *first*.

> Starting their first road trip of the season.

This group of words does not make sense. In reading the two sentences forward, you probably read them as one instead of two. That's why you may have had a difficult time spotting the fragment beginning with the **ING word** *starting*.

Remember, when you are proofreading your composition to check for fragments, begin by reading your assignments backwards in reverse order one sentence at a time. Pause after each sentence. If it doesn't sound right, check to see if it includes a **glue word**, **WH word**, or **ING word**.

EXERCISE 2: Now try some trickier practice. Some of the examples below are lonesome fragments because they are chopped off from the first part of the sentence. On a separate sheet of paper, number your paper from 1 to 10. Write FRAG if the group is a fragment. Some examples are correctly combined using **glue words**, **WH words**, and **ING words**. Write OK after these sentence numbers.

1. I'm meeting my cousin Bertha later today. At the city swimming pool.
2. Two baby crabs scurried to hide. Under a wet rock on the beach.
3. The mountain roads curved down, passing wide lakes, tall trees, and high cliffs.
4. Jane earns extra money. Training bumble bees to play slide trombones.
5. A silver-tipped hawk glided down to Randy. Who had raised it from birth.
6. Snacking Sidney spread peanut butter and marshmallow sauce on burnt toast.
7. Smiling yellow daisies are growing tall. Beside the railroad tracks outside of town.
8. Winston wagged his tail. When Cornflakes landed on his head.
9. Milton and Warren skateboarded to school, falling down only seven times.
10. I ordered a tall stack of pancakes. Which I couldn't finish eating.

95

EXERCISE 3: Ready for some more practice? Number your paper from 1 to 10. Write FRAG or OK after each number. Correct all fragments.

1. We sat on the subway near a man. Who howled with laughter.
2. Babs brushes her hamster's teeth using a pipe cleaner.
3. A few elderly elephants have rolled over. Onto my side of the bed.
4. Miserable Max bricked up the door to his bedroom. So that no one could enter.
5. The crew of sailors was fast asleep beneath the ship's deck.
6. "Oh, no!" cried Roberto in shock. Watching his pet guinea pig hop off on his pogo stick.
7. Patty jammed on the brakes to stop in time, which was all she could do.
8. I asked Nancy to put my lunch money inside her purse for me.
9. The McNutty family wants to stop for a rest. Where there is a picnic table.
10. Danielle smiled to herself. As her canary sang sweet songs.

FRAGMENT TIP NUMBER 3

A great way to check for fragments is to use the following trick. Read the words **I BELIEVE THAT** before the sentence you are checking. If it sounds okay, it is probably a complete thought. If it sounds confusing, it is probably a fragment.

I BELIEVE THAT

Galloping turtles are a figment of your imagination.

I BELIEVE THAT galloping turtles are a figment of your imagination.

This sounds okay, so it's not a fragment.

However, if you add the words **I BELIEVE THAT** before a sentence fragment, then the new sentence will sound confusing. This is your immediate clue that a fragment has crept into your writing.

Galloping into the night with the rest of them.

I BELIEVE THAT galloping into the night with the rest of them.

This doesn't make sense, does it? Therefore, it's time to fix that fragment. How would you repair it?

DIFFICULT TO SPOT FRAGMENTS

You should know that not all fragments begin with **glue words**, **WH words**, and **ING words**. Some fragments are not so easily spotted. These fragments are only missing one part of one idea.

Here is one idea that was stretched:

> The prestidigitator who juggles golf balls accidentally swallowed one.

Of course, the main idea is:

> The prestidigitator swallowed one. (golf ball)
> Doer   Did   What

If either part of the sentence is missing, the Doer or the Did, it is a fragment.

> The prestidigitator who juggles golf balls   FRAG

> Accidentally swallowed one   FRAG

Here is another idea which has been stretched:

> A possum snoozes.
> Doer   Does

> A big, fat possum lazily snoozes on our roof.
> Doer   Does   Where

If either the Doer or Does is chopped off, the lonesome part remaining is a fragment.

> A big, fat possum   FRAG
> Doer needs a Does.

> lazily snoozes on our roof   FRAG
> Does needs a Doer.

EXERCISE 4: Your turn now. Study the paragraph which follows. Some of the numbered sentences are fragments because they lack either the Doer or the Does/Did part of the sentence. Number your paper 1 to 15. Write FRAG after the number of each fragment you spot. Why not try the **I BELIEVE THAT** tip with this practice?

Harold the Hot Dog

1. Handsome Harold with big, blue eyes. 2. Strolled around the sunny swimming pool. 3. Harold wore fancy glasses to protect his eyes. 4. Would be squinting uncomfortably without the sunglasses on. 5. Always wore them at poolside. 6. The high-diving tower with fifty-nine steps. 7. Reflected off Harold's sunglasses, drawing his attention. 8. With rippling muscles he strode toward the ladder. 9. Grabbing the handrails firmly. 10. In smooth motions he climbed to the top. 11. The suntanned diver, whose oiled body glistened. 12. Posed dramatically on the platform. 13. Springing like a carrier plane from a catapult. 14. Soaring in a swan dive, he remembered something was wrong. 15. Quickly tucking and cannon balling to avoid smashing his sunglasses into his big, blue eyes.

EXERCISE 5: Here's some extra practice for fragment finders. Tell what is missing, the Doer or the Did.

1. Was licking his chops happily after wolfing down seven Big Macs.
2. My very favorite color in blouses is.
3. Needlessly slammed the screen door of the cabin.
4. Stretched across the bright, blue sky in a straight line.
5. Cousin Connie from Saskatoon.
6. Leaped tall buildings in a single bound.
7. Had climbed up the bird cage to see what was for lunch.
8. A band of marching trumpet players from the school.

CORRECTING FRAGMENTS

Now that you have had some practice finding fragments, it is time to try correcting them. Since fragments prevent writing ideas in complete sentences, it will be helpful for you to learn how to correct them. Actually, it's easy enough. **Expand** with the missing information using journalistic questions.

Here, for instance, is a fragment.

> While I wrote my story.

To correct the fragment, answer the unanswered question about what was going on while you wrote the story.

> While I wrote my story, **Vince pretended he was Tarzan**.

> or

> **My foot fell asleep under the desk** while I wrote my story.

> or

> **Maxwell, our cat, took a nap on my head** while I wrote my story.

> or

While I wrote my story,_____.

An Easy Composing Rule

USING A COMMA TO SET OFF AN INTRODUCTORY CLAUSE

While we're exploring this whole business of fragments, it's probably also a good time to introduce a new composing rule about commas. Go back and look at the example sentence in the section before this. Here's the sentence.

> While I wrote my story, Vince pretended he was Tarzan.

By looking carefully, you can see that the **GLUE** fragment (*While I wrote my story*) was added onto the rest of the sentence (*Vince pretended he was Tarzan.*) By hooking the **GLUE** fragment to the rest of the sentence, a new, complete sentence is formed. However, in order to do this correctly, you can see that the writer used a comma to set off the **GLUE** fragment or clause.

You can see this same pattern in the following two sentences.

> Running to catch my bus, I tripped on my untied shoe laces.
> (Comma sets off an **ING** phrase)

> Because she double dribbled all the time, she continued to turn the ball over.
> (Comma sets off a **GLUE WORD** clause)

COMMA RULE 6

These examples all show a new rule of punctuation, another comma rule.

> When an **ING** phrase, a **GLUE WORD** clause or a **WH WORD** clause **begins** a sentence, it needs to be followed (set off by) a comma.

EXERCISE 6: Correct these fragments. Identify their unanswered questions and **expand**. Remember the comma rule we just reviewed. If any of your new sentences begin with a **WH WORD**, and **ING WORD** or a **GLUE WORD**, check to make sure that you have set that clause or phrase off with a comma.

> *Example:* In order to rescue the family's porcupine.

What would the reader ask after reading these words?

What had to be done in order to rescue the family's porcupine?

> *Answer:* **In order to rescue the family's porcupine**, Dad and Uncle Chester dragged the ladder to the porch.

Notice that order of the sentence was moved around above to add the comma.

1. Beneath my math book.
2. Leaving his ticket book back at Pancho's Diner.
3. Who raised it from birth.
4. When Cornflakes landed on his head.
5. Onto my side of the bed.
6. Watching his pet guinea pig ride off on his pogo stick.
7. Beside the railroad tracks outside of town.
8. Even though they were aiming for the swimming pool.
9. Which is the secret step in the recipe.
10. Training bumble bees to play slide trombones.

EXERCISE 7: Correct these lonesome fragments by looking back a few pages to **EXERCISES 3** and **4** to find their missing Doer or Does sentence parts. Remember to use a capital letter and end punctuation.

1. The prestidigitator who juggles golf balls.
2. Lazily snoozes on our roof.
3. Handsome Harold with big, blue eyes.
4. The high-diving tower with fifty-nine steps.
5. So that no one could enter.

EXERCISE 8: Correct the following fragments by expanding. Let your imagination gallop as you have fun doing so. Remember the comma rule for any introductory clause or phrase. Let's see how different solutions work.

1. Dancing around the room with a broom.
2. Onto its woolly back.
3. Who howls with laughter.
4. Because of one, huge cavity.
5. The Red Rodents, who hadn't won a game all year.
6. Eating scraps from the dining room table.
7. That someone else had made in art.
8. When the lights went out in the cabin.
9. Between my tire and the sidewalk.
10. Hiding beneath her table.

11. Irma Irving with gold hair and teeth.
12. Gargled with mouthwash every morning.
13. Seven thousand excuses every time.
14. Joyfully jumped through the juniper weeds.
15. More than a few eels.
16. Couldn't have been careful.
17. Hadn't remembered to turn off the water.
18. After Sweet William scored the winning goal.
19. An old, smelly package inside the hallway closet.
20. Dennie Denton, the furnace repairman.

Have you ever tried to explain what happened in your school's cafeteria during Spirit Week? Or how you talked your way out of a detention? Or how you convinced your dad into raising your allowance? There are many times when you will want to tell about something which has happened in your past.

Obviously, you will want the reader to know that all the action has been completed, even though he may be hearing about it for the first time. Therefore, you are going to write a memory paper in the past tense.

Also, in order to make your listener feel he was there with you, you will paint your memory picture with words. Use your senses to recall details.

Finally, since this will be your memory, you will write the paper in the first person singular. This is the *I*, *me*, *my*, and *mine* point of view. You will be telling someone about something which happened to you.

STAGE ONE: PREWRITING

STUDENT LEARNING OBJECTIVES

1. The student will narrate a personal memory which has a beginning, middle, and end.
2. The student will limit the memory in space, time/action and character(s).
3. The student will use first person pronouns and past tense verbs to tell the experience.
4. The student will **combine** and/or **expand** to create interesting sentences.
5. The student will avoid fragments.

WHERE DO I START?

On the next page is a student-model memory paper which describes something that has already happened. By reading this paper, you can get a better idea about the past tense and first person pronouns.

The Headache

1. Angrily I **steamed** into my darkened room. **2.** I **tossed** my books on the desk.

3. Hating its message, I **hid** the horrible report card under my pillow. **4.** With one hand

I **adjusted** my tearstained glasses. **5.** With the other hand I **stroked** my messy hair.

6. As I **clenched** my fists tightly, I almost **smelled** the school blackboards. **7.** The

thought of school only **caused** a headache. **8.** I put an album on the stereo. **9.** My

overhead light **made** my pacing shadow appear to move jerkily. **10.** I **felt** a strange

buzzing in my head. **11.** Bright lights **seemed** to be dancing around me. **12.** I **floated**

on the waves of the music, which **pounded** from the twin speakers. **13.** Every muscle in

my body **surrendered** to the beat of the music. **14.** My thoughts now **centered** on

the music instead of the failure notice. **15.** Time **stood** still.

In this paragraph there is one main clue which tells you that this action has already been completed and is now being remembered. That clue is the fact that most of the verbs end in **-ed**, which indicates the past tense. Such verbs are all regular verbs because they always end in **-ed**.

Not all past tense verbs end in **-ed**, however. Some others are called irregular verbs because the past tense is not formed in the regular manner. In the model paragraph the verb, **stood**, is an example of this type of irregular past tense verb. Can you pick out other irregular past tense verbs from **The Headache**?

HELPFUL DRILL 1--EXAMINING A PAST TENSE PAPER

Look at the model paragraph, **The Headache**. Reread it aloud to yourself. Look and listen for past tense verbs.

After rereading it, fill out the following question sheet on a separate piece of paper. Answering these questions will help you prepare to write your own memory paper.

The Headache Question Sheet

1. What was the memory that the writer described?
2. How much time passed?
3. Where did the action take place?
4. Who was the main character? Expand your description! Be specific.
5. Using the subject-verb chart below, list all the personal pronouns (I, me, mine, my) used to identify the Doer. Also, list all verbs used to describe what the Doer did. In the last column, count the number of words in each sentence. Do this for each numbered sentence in **The Headache**.

SUBJECT/VERB CHART: THE HEADACHE

DOER/SUBJECT	DID/VERBS	# OF WORDS
1.		
2.		
3.		
4.		
5.		
6.		
7.		
8.		
9.		
10.		
11.		
12.		
13.		
14.		
15.		

6. Which sentence begins with an **ING** opening?
7. Which sentences begin with **glue words**?
8. How many verbs ended in **ed**?
9. Which verbs did not end in **ed**? Why?

HELPFUL DRILL 2--PRACTICING AS A GROUP

Before you begin to write your own memory paper, it may be helpful for your entire class or your cooperative learning groups to practice a little more with this type of writing. Use the story starter as a beginning. Then complete memory paragraphs using only past tense verbs.

> In order to save an extra mile of walking, I took a shortcut through the cemetery on Halloween. I had to be home by ten o'clock; it was already 9:45 p.m. I knew my folks would worry if I were late.

Instructions for Group and Cooperative Learning Teams

To help get started, use the following strategies for the class or your cooperative learning group.

1. First, decide what happens in the beginning, middle and end of this short experience. Remember that you want to get into this quickly, develop suspense in the middle and finish with a snappy ending. As a class, discuss this and have your teacher diagram the action on the board. Come up with only two or three possibilities for each section and then choose the best.

2. Next, break up into teams of three. Each team will be assigned to work on the beginning, middle or end. They should make a list of items or vocabulary words which might be included in their particular section. After ten minutes of brainstorming, share the lists and choose the best items for the class overall. Remember that you want to move the action along, but also make it easier to *see* what is being described.

3. Finally, when your teacher has finished listing all the ideas on the board, you will again work in cooperative teams of three. Using the general outline on the board, one of you will write the beginning of this narrative, one the middle, and one the end. Each section should be about one paragraph long. When each is finished with the rough draft, compare and fit together all three paragraphs into one complete paper. You may have to do some editing to make everything flow together.

   Most papers will be shared in class.

   When you have finished your class-composed papers, use the questions from **The Headache Question Sheet**, page 105, to study what you have written.

106

USING STRONG IDEAS AND CONTENT TO HELP YOUR PAPERS

It's almost time to start your own paper here. However, before you jump in, let's spend just a minute emphasizing another trait you can use to improve your writing. The memory paper that you will write shortly, will allow you to use your own **ideas and experiences.** You know from your own reading that papers or stories are much more interesting and fun if they contain content that is creative or original. Ideas in a paper can also be engaging if somehow you can relate to what is being written. Can you see a little of yourself in the story?

In order to develop good **ideas and content,** one of the most important traits in writing, then you need to ask yourself these questions.

1. Does my paper have something interesting or important to say?
2. Have I used clear details or experiences to make my reader feel involved?
3. Do I stick to my topic and not go off on tangents?
4. If I read my own paper, could I stay interested in the topic?

As you begin to explore the subject for you own paper, ask yourself these questions. Remember, **ideas and content** are the foundation of paper. Without great ideas, your paper will not satisfy you or your reader.

WRITING PROMPT

For your own topic, you are going to describe some memory from your past. It's important that you come up with a memory which you can recall very well. Use these questions to help you remember:

1. Looking back over the years, can you remember a time when you were . . .

very embarrassed	scared	tempted
angry	hot--freezing	frustrated
nervous	cold--sweating	crying
shy	angry	thankful
curious	giggly	sympathctic

2. Have you ever been with any of your friends when you felt any of the above feelings or emotions?

Why not share memories that might be an excellent topic for this assignment?

From your brainstorming of your past memories, come up with one good memory which can be described in a brief paper--no more than two or three paragraphs in length. Remember this should be something where the action happens very quickly and then is over.

Before you write, complete the following **Think Sheet** to help collect all your ideas.

MEMORY PAPER THINK SHEET

1. What is the memory you are writing about?

2. Are there any characters besides yourself in the memory? If so, who?

3. Where does the remembered event take place?

4. How much time passed?

5. **VERY IMPORTANT!** In the space below, please draw a picture/map of your memory and include as many of the details as you can remember when you close your eyes and try to recall this event. Drawing ability is not important, but details are!

6. Now, jot down your recollections of the events that happened in each section. Use all your senses.

	Actions	Specific Details
The beginning		
The middle		
The end		

STAGE TWO: WRITING THE FIRST DRAFT

Here are some final reminders about the writing of a good memory paper. Think about them before you start writing your first draft.

1. Limit the memory topic to a specific place and an equally specific time/action frame.
2. Plunge right into your description of the action.
3. Make sure your paper has a beginning, a middle, and an ending.
4. **Expand** with supportive details. Use your senses.
5. All verbs must be in the past tense--the *yesterday* tense.
6. Try to glue your sentences together in various ways.
7. Vary your sentence openings.
8. Do not write fragments.

Remember, address ideas first, then mechanics. You cannot do a good job with both at the same time.

Write your first draft with your **Think Sheet** as your guide. One final check on **The Headache** model could help. Number each sentence, and skip a line between each written line of your paragraph. You will use the in-between lines for corrections.

SENTENCE OPENING SHEET (SOS)--HELP SHEET

Once you have written your first draft, you will fill out the **Sentence Opening Sheet** for this paper.

For each numbered sentence you will provide the information called for in the instructions which follow.

Column 1	**Sentence Openings:**	Write down the first four words of each sentence.
Column 2	**First Person Pronouns:**	Write down each Doer pronoun. Each should be in some form of the first person.
Column 3	**Verbs:**	Write down the verbs.
Column 4	**# of Words:**	Write down the number of words in each sentence.

To help you get the picture of how you will use the **SOS**, follow your teacher as **The Headache** paragraph is modeled for **SOS** purposes.

As you study your **Sentence Opening Sheet**, ask yourself these questions about the various columns:

QUESTIONS FOR COLUMN 1

1. Are there different sentence openings?
2. Do all of my sentences begin with the words *I* or *The*?
3. Could I make my sentences more interesting by **combining** some of them so that I do not start too many of them with the same opening?
4. Do any of my sentences begin with **ING words**? **glue words**? **WH words**? Are these sentences actually fragments?

QUESTIONS FOR COLUMN 2

1. Are all of my Doer pronouns in the first person?
2. If any of the Doer pronouns are not in the first person, fix them.

QUESTIONS FOR COLUMN 3

1. Are all the verbs that I identified in the past tense?
2. Could I make my paper more interesting by using more specific or colorful verbs instead of repeating the same verbs over and over?

QUESTIONS FOR COLUMN 4

1. Are any of my overly long sentences really more than one sentence run together?
2. Do I include too many short, choppy sentences?

Special Helper: Remember! The purpose of the **Sentence Opening Sheet** is to help you spot items which may need to be corrected. You can make these changes on your rough draft and in your final draft.

You do not need to complete a **Sentence Opening Sheet** for your final draft.

STAGE THREE: REWRITING

In the rewriting stage you should correct all the mistakes on the first draft, using the **Sentence Opening Sheet** and the feedback you receive from a proofreading partner.

Try to make your final draft error free. Reread it and have someone else read your paper aloud. Quite often this will help you hear mistakes which you otherwise might have missed.

Before you start proofreading, brush up on your skills. Using this student first draft, see if you can spot the errors in this model.

The Cookies

1. I quietly slipped through the sliding door. **2.** We look around and see the large tray of rich chocolate chip cookies on the table. **3.** Before I knew it, my hand reached out and scooped up three of the cookies. **4.** Slowly lifted my hand to my mouth. **5.** The cookies smelled wonderful. **6.** With a deliberate motion I bit into the first cookie and utter a sigh of satisfaction. **7.** I decide that six cookies would taste twice as good as three. **8.** I help myself to three more. **9.** Grinning, I turn to leave. **10.** Mom is standing at the door.

1. In which sentences does the writer slip from past tense into the present, a *no-no* in this assignment? Correct these mistakes.

2. In which sentence does the writer shift away from the first person singular? Correct this sentence.

3. Identify the fragment. Correct it.

CHECKLIST SHEET

As you read your partner's paper, fill in the **Checklist Sheet**. When your partner returns your own paper and the **Checklist Sheet**, you will be ready to revise your final work. Consider all the feedback you are given. Write the final draft of your memory paper.

MEMORY PAPER CHECKLIST

1. What is the memory being described?

2. How much time passed?

3. Where did the memory take place?

4. Does the memory clearly contain a beginning, a middle, and an ending? (On the writer's first draft, indicate the beginning with a *B*, the middle with an *M*, and the ending with an *E*.)

5. If the beginning, middle, and ending are not interesting, give some specific hints to the writer by asking the journalistic questions **who**, **what**, **when**, **where**, **why**, and **how**.

6. Are all the writer's verbs in the past tense? If not, correct them on the first draft.

7. Does the writer repeat the same verbs over and over again? If he does, give him suggestions on the first draft.

8. Does the writer vary his sentence openings?

9. Mark any fragments with FRAG.

10. What one thing could most improve this paper?

11. What was the best feature of the paper?

STAGE FOUR: PUBLISHING

Finish the final draft of the memory paper using your best penmanship. Make a cover for your paper, by putting some finishing touches on the drawing from your **Think Sheet**.

Consider making a class book with everyone's memory paper. Several would probably be good to share aloud!

Another good idea would be to set aside class time just to share memory papers. No comments of any kind are needed. Just be a good listener.

Oral Language into Writing

CREATING NEW WORDS

Our language gives names to things and actions around us so we can talk about them. Instead of having to say, "I rode my *piece of metal with two rubber tires, a seat, and curved metal steering bar* to the beach," we can say, "I rode my *bicycle* to the beach." Much easier, right?

People are always inventing names for things and actions. For example, someone decided that a good name for a car or bicycle tire that was punctured would be a *flat tire*, or *flat* for short. Likewise, when kids began to accelerate their motorcycles and bikes so that the front tire lifted off the ground, someone called it a *wheelie*.

Unfortunately, not everything we use or do has an English name. For example, the creamy white frosting inside an Oreo cookie has no name. Fortunately, Rich Hall has decided to give it a much deserved name: he calls it *re*.

In fact, he has written a whole book about new words, called **Sniglets**. (**Any Word that Doesn't Appear in the Dictionary, but Should**, Macmillan Publishing Company, 1990.)

Here are some more sniglets, or new names, Rich created:

meouch: the part of a cat's neck that you're allowed to grab and lift although the cat never seems to think it's okay

shoecide: one abandoned shoe in the road

petaphor: any metaphor or simile that uses an animal in it (such as *sick as a dog* or *quick like a fox*)

Pretty clever! Notice how the author tried to use parts of the old names to make his new names.

In *meouch* he took the *me* from *meow* and added it to *ouch*.

He used the *cide* from *suicide* and connected it to *shoe* to form the new sniglet *shoecide*.

The new word, *petaphor*, came from *pet* and *metaphor*.

WARM-UP ACTIVITY 1

Match these *things* with their new names.

1. a notebook that breaks open onto the floor		a. scrooch
2. pencil with no eraser left on top		b balder
3. sound a skateboard makes when the wheels are turned sharply		c. blub
4. a piece of Scotch tape peeled off to be used again		d. bindbreaker
5. a burned-out lightbulb		e. Botch tape

HOW TO CREATE NEW NAMES

New names are fun to invent. You probably already have created words in your everyday language. All you do is use your imagination to make up a name that fits a thing. Look how the words from **Warm-up Activity 1** were created:

1. make a compound word	(bind + breaker)
2. describe its looks	(balder)
3. describe its sound	(scrooch)
4. use parts of old	(*botch* from *to botch something* and *tape* from *Scotch tape*)
5 invent a funny-sounding word	(blub)

WARM-UP ACTIVITY 2

Invent new names for these common things. The class can decide which student invented the best new name for each one.

1. a piece of notebook paper with all three holes torn out
2. the *fast walk* used by a student slowing down when she notices a teacher watching her run in the hall
3. the last piece of ice stuck at the bottom of a cup that won't tap loose
4. a marking pen that has dried out because you forgot to cap it
5. a lonely sock in your drawer that doesn't match any other

6. the act of pretending to be asleep when someone enters your bedroom to check on you
7. a stapler that is out of staples
8. the embarrassment you feel when you're laughing loudly and then everyone else suddenly stops
9. the tiny pieces of broken glass along the road waiting to puncture your bike's tires
10. a tube of toothpaste that has been squeezed from the middle instead of properly rolled up from the bottom

WARM-UP ACTIVITY 3

With your cooperative learning group, make up two new sniglets. Vote on the group that creates the *best* sniglets. You might want to draw a creative picture of our sniglet.

RUN-ON SENTENCES

Now we will deal with the most common problem in student writing: the infamous, dreaded, notorious RUN-ON SENTENCES. These have been mentioned briefly before.

Of all the problems young writers face, run-ons are *numero uno*. Often it is the worst composition problem for junior high school students, high school students, many college students, and even some adults. BUT NOT TO WORRY. You will now learn to spot and eliminate the unwanted, miserable, wicked RO's forever!!

Here is what typically happens: Sometimes, when sentences are combined, **glue words** or **connectors** are forgotten. This results in sentences running together. These *runny* sentences are called run-on sentences, or RO's, for short.

Read this example aloud:

> The family hunted for turtles they found many near the lake.

What are the two sentences that run together? Without a **glue word** or **connector** to combine these sentences, a run-on sentence, a RO, results.

EXERCISE 1: Here are some examples of run-on sentences. Tell what the two sentences are. It helps to read the sentences *aloud*. Hearing them helps to recognize RO's.

1. Mom and Dad groaned the repair bill for the dryer was $130.
2. Fred dashed behind the barrel Janet scrambled up a tree.
3. A black spider smiles to itself a careless fly zooms toward his web.
4. Mr. Birosak from Tunaville packed his suitcase he forgot his hairpiece on the bed.
5. Akeem raced sixteen blocks home he was late for dinner.
6. A young duck floated in the moat the crocodiles played water polo.
7. Little Walter blew his harmonica the band blasted music behind him.
8. A pair of eggs sizzled in the frying pan the smell reached the camper's nose.
9. The bucket leaks water drips out.
10. Frances arrowed her bow the wolf stood frozen in the night.

EXERCISE 2: Are you getting the feel for recognizing run-ons? Your goal is to eliminate them. Try some more examples. Read the sentences *aloud* to hear the run-ons. What are the two sentences?

1. The one-legged pirate shaved his whiskers the mirror cracked in surprise.
2. Delvin munched tacos he drank a coke.
3. Marta clipped her toenails she whistled a happy tune.
4. This family of geese must love stale bread it has eaten two loaves already.
5. Dixie dozed at her desk her boss didn't even notice.

6. That mountain bike needs repair it is missing both its brakes and a seat.
7. Kai dove in head first the pool's water felt like the Arctic Ocean.
8. The big snake thought about lunch a mouse or two seemed just perfect.
9. Jo knows karate she uses it only in self defense.
10. The rubber raft rushed down the river each rider hung on with both hands.

CUT A STRING OF RUN-ONS

Here are some more exercises in picking out run-ons. You should be getting better and better in hearing them.

EXERCISE 3: Now it's time to recognize run-ons that have been strung together in a paragraph about Dr. Frank Posner, a dentist from Colorado. There are twenty sentences in this paragraph. On a separate sheet of paper, number from 1 to 20. List the first word and the last word of each sentence. Also, write the letter of the line (a-n) in which the first word of each sentence appears.

He Needed a Vacation

a. In early August Dr. Frank Posner needed a vacation badly he was

b. tired out from hard work at his dental office buying an airplane ticket

c. he flew to a far-away town in Oregon there he visited two old friends

d. each night all three stayed up late they talked and talked about the

e. good old days early in the morning his friends promptly arose from

f. bed to go jogging tired Frank stayed in bed after a few days Frank

g. became curious about their jogging he wondered how people could

h. actually get up early to run and sweat the next day Frank decided to

i. join them huffing and puffing, Frank struggled to keep up he didn't

j. give up though the next morning he went jogging again by the end of

k. a week Frank was beginning to like it his endurance increased each

l. day he began to feel better he began to think ahead about entering

m. the Boston Marathon his two friends were proud of Frank little did

n. they know Frank was planning on jogging home instead of flying!

CORRECTING RUN-ONS WITH ING, WH, AND GLUE WORDS

After you know how to recognize run-ons, the next step is to learn how to correct them. The goal is for you to eliminate run-ons from your own writing. If you see a run-on in your paper, it's easy to correct. You will learn three ways of doing so.

Let's turn to the family we left on page 118, hunting for turtles:

> The family hunted for turtles they found many near the lake.

This run-on has two sentences running together. They are easily corrected. Just add **ING words**, **WH words**, or **glue words**.

> **1.** The family hunted for turtles, **finding** many near the lake. (ING)
> **2.** The family **that** hunted for turtles found many near the lake. (WH)
> **3.** **As** the family hunted for turtles, they found many near the lake. (glue)

Here is another run-on which needs repair.

> Jumping Joe leaped over the fence he landed in the hog wallow.

This run-on is corrected by adding an **ING word**.

> Jumping Joe leaped over the fence, *landing* in the hog wallow.

It can also be corrected using a **WH word**.

> Jumping Joe, *who* leaped over the fence, landed in the hog wallow.

A **glue word** can also be used.

> *When* Jumping Joe leaped over the fence, he landed in the hog wallow.

EXERCISE 4: Correct these run-ons by adding **ING words**, **WH words**, and **glue words**.

> **1 .** Samantha sang sweet songs she was picking posies in the pasture.
> **a.** Samantha sang sweet songs, _____ posies in the pasture. (ING)
> **b.** Samantha, _____ sang sweet songs, was picking posies in the pasture. (WH)
> **c.** Samantha sang sweet songs _____ picking posies in the pasture. (glue)

2. Rollo completed his art project he watched the Nets game.
   a. Rollo completed his art project, _____ the Nets game.
   b. Rollo, _____ completed his art project, watched the Nets game.
   c. Rollo completed his art project _____ he watched the Nets game.

3. The Brahma bull knocked Tex down it charged out of the corral.
   a. The Brahma bull knocked Tex down, _____ out of the corral.
   b. The Brahma bull, _____ knocked Tex down, charged out of the corral.
   c. The Brahma bull knocked Tex down _____ charging out of the corral.

4. Del was swatting flies he used his homework as a swatter.
   a. Del was swatting flies, _____ his homework as a swatter.
   b. Del, _____ swatted flies, used his homework as a swatter.
   c. _____ Del was swatting flies, he used his homework as a swatter.

5. The beaver gnawed on logs she cut them like a chain saw.
   a. The beaver gnawed on logs, _____ them like a chain saw.
   b. The beaver, _____ gnawed on logs, cut them like a chain saw.
   c. _____ the beaver gnawed on logs, she cut them like a chain saw.

YOUR ATTENTION PLEASE: A comma (,) is not glue. When two sentences are joined using just a comma, it is a RO--- **known as a *comma splice*.**

EXERCISE 5: Do you still have enough glue left? You will need some to fix these runny run-ons. Pick **glue words**, **ING words**, or **WH words** to correct the run-ons.

1. Dolores naps in the bay window, she dreams of sardine sandwiches.
2. The king's castle appeared before us, dark clouds covered the pointy towers of the battlements.
3. Oswald the otter paddles breathlessly across the pond, he spotted a fox on the bank.
4. Our friend did magic tricks, she vanished her younger brother, Robbie.
5. Rhonda Rockette set the school record, she ran the 60-yard dash in 9.5 seconds.
6. A few crumbs tumbled from the picnic table, a scouting party of ants noticed.
7. I've learned to save water, I now wash the supper dishes by hand.
8. Herman the Vermin creeps through the cellar, he avoids mousetraps.
9. A gold streak of sunlight peeked through the clouds, raindrops stopped falling.
10. Rolando finished his violin lesson, he hurried outside to his bike.

CORRECTING RUN-ONS WITH *BOYS FAN* WORDS

Here is still another way to correct run-on sentences:

Maxi the Taxi sped through traffic it was time to return to the garage.
Maxi the Taxi sped through traffic, **for** it was time to return to the garage.

This **glue word** is called a connector word.

Here is a list of **connector words**, also called coordinating conjunctions:

BUT = contrast, on the contrary
OR = options
YET = nevertheless
SO = results   *BOYS   FAN*
FOR = because or since
AND = addition
NOR = negative alternative

EXERCISE 6: First, find the **BOYS FAN** word in each sentence. Copy the word before it, copy the **BOYS FAN** word, and copy the word after it. Then, put a comma in front of the connector word. Finally, underline the **BOYS FAN** word.

Example: Early in the morning I wake up so I can read the comics.
up, <u>so</u> I

1. Fred dashed behind the barrel so Janet scrambled up the tree.
2. Mr. Birosak packs his suitcase but he forgets his hairpiece on the bed.
3. A young crocodile floats in the swamp and the water is murky.
4. Delbert doesn't eat peanuts yet he eats the shells.
5. This bucket is leaking or the floor was already wet.

EXERCISE 7: Use **BOYS FAN** words to rewrite these run-on sentences. Pick the connector which best glues the two ideas together. Each of the seven **BOYS FAN** words has a slightly different meaning.

1. Ravenous Ravenal snatched up the last French fry I ate the rest of the hamburger.
2. The angry driver blew his horn the Mustang in front of him was dallying at the stoplight.
3. Senta works days in a hot dog joint at night she washes cars at the car wash.
4. That herd of rhinos will check into the Bighorn Motel they will continue to gallop down the interstate highway.
5. Hazel and Henrietta grow radishes in their garden they hate to eat them.
6. Tulip Tanski, the class president, called the meeting to order it was time to begin.

CORRECT RUN-ONS BY REWRITING THE SENTENCES

Run-on sentences can be corrected still another way. You can rewrite the sentences separately.

Here is a long, rambling, run-on sentence.

> The yellow skirt that Clara loaned me last Thursday for the school play was faded very badly tiny threads, looking like starving worms, hung loosely from top to bottom.

Notice that when they are split into two separate sentences, the first sentence is followed by the end punctuation. The second sentence begins with a capital letter.

> The yellow skirt that Clara loaned me last Thursday for the school play was faded very badly. Tiny threads, looking like starving worms, hung loosely from top to bottom.

EXERCISE 8: Each of the numbered sets of sentences below contains run-ons. Number a sheet of paper 1a and 1b, 2a and 2b, and so on. Alongside the appropriate sentence number, list the first and last word of each run-on you correct when you separate it into two sentences.

1. Fourteen, open-top cages of lions were lined up side by side behind a take-off ramp at the other end Daredevil Debra, wearing black leather pants, jacket, and gloves, revved up her shiny, black motorcycle at the end of the runway.

2. The hungry lions, which hadn't eaten in two days, paced back and forth silently in their cages Debra's black suit would be less than the protective peel on a banana to such lions.

3. The grandstands, packed full of screaming fans, sagged under the weight all eyes peered down the pavement toward the lonely figure in black.

4. Carefully placing a black racing helmet on her head, Debra was thinking about her touchdown on the landing ramp beyond the cages even though flying over the fourteen caged lions would be easy, keeping her balance as she hit the second ramp would be the hard part.

5. Settling onto the motorcycle saddle, Debra carefully adjusted her racing goggles over her eyes with a scream of power the motorcycle roared down the runway toward the take-off ramp, and the lions roared in answer to the bike.

WRITING WARM UP

FRAGMENT AND RUN-ON FINALE

EXERCISE 9: As the grand finale to the sentence fragment and run-on sentence exercises in **Units 5** and **6**, read the following paragraph. Then identify the fragments and run-ons. Rewrite the paragraph on a separate sheet of paper, correcting these two major types of student errors.

Man's Best Friend

1. When the clock in the town hall tower struck two o'clock in the morning. **2.** Jimbo was almost home. **3.** Turning down Euclid Avenue. **4.** He threw the Nissan into neutral he coasted to a quiet stop in front of the house. **5.** He smiled in relief all the lights in the house were turned off a dark house meant his folks were asleep. **6.** If he sneaked in successfully. **7.** They might never find out he'd missed his one o'clock curfew. **8.** They told him he would lose his Friday night privileges for a month. **9.** Whenever he was late coming home. **10.** With his fingers crossed for good luck. **11.** He opened and shut the front door without making a sound.

12. As he tiptoed up the carpeted stairs.

13. Jimbo's dog Pal started barking loud enough to wake up the dead and Jimbo's father, a light sleeper at best, was far from dead, and so of course he woke up too and noticed what time it was.

14. While a happy Pal joyously greeted his master.

15. Jimbo wondered why they called the dog man's best friend.

Major Writing Assignment

In order to get the most out of life, you need to be a careful observer. If a policeman or fireman or pilot were not careful observers, what type of problems could occur? What about your everyday life? When, where, and how do you need to be a careful observer?

In this next paper, the observation paper, you will be describing an event as if it were unfolding right before your eyes. Unlike the memory paper, you want the reader to feel as if he is right there with you as you observe the event.

For example, suppose you are an observer at an international cross-country ski championship. Hedy Heinz is in the middle of the ten-kilometer race course. She is skiing across the side of a hill along a narrow track. Above her is a thick, pine forest. Below her is a steep, icy drop-off. As Hedy pauses to catch her breath, you see a bear crash out of the forest, startling her.

Read the following observation which you, as the observer, might have written to report what happened. The present verbs are all **bold**.

The Terrified Skier

1. Under a large, pine tree Hedy Heinz **pauses** to catch her breath. **2.** She **looks** at the thick, pine forest above the narrow ski track, which **goes** along the side of the hill. **3.** She quickly **notes** the steep, icy drop-off below the track. **4.** At first she **hears** nothing but the pounding of her own heart. **5.** Then, making low, grunting noises, a large bear **crashes** through the underbrush. **6.** Frightened, Hedy **glances** at the advancing bear. **7.** She **is** even more frightened as she **considers** the drop-off. **8.** Her heart **beats** 180. **9.** The bear **stands** on his hind legs and **coughs** his warning. **10.** The ice and bare rocks below Hedy silently **give** their warning. **11.** She **knows** she **can**not **pole** ahead to escape the bear. **12.** She **makes** the hard choice. **13.** The cross-country skier **becomes** a downhill skier. **14.** Screaming in fear, Hedy **hurtles** down the steep drop-off. **15.** She **flashes** through the scrub trees, and the pine needles **whip** her face. **16.** Her skis **do** not **bite** the ice as she **tries** to change direction to avoid a rock. **17.** She **falls** heavily and **slides** into a snowbank in a jumble of bent poles and tangled skis. **18.** The bear **observes** her curiously and then **ambles** off along the cross-country ski track.

125

STAGE ONE: PREWRITING

STUDENT LEARNING OBJECTIVES

1. The student will write a *you are there*--observation paper which includes a beginning, a middle, and an ending.
2. The student will use the voice of an announcer describing what she/he observes.
3. The student will plunge immediately into the action.
4. The student will use only the third person pronouns.
5. The student will limit the paper in space, time/action, and character(s).
6. The student will write all verbs in the present tense.
7. The student will avoid run-ons.
8. The student will include one original *new* word.

FOCUSED WRITING TRAITS

Good writers are those who have mastered the *traits* of quality writing. Traits are the characteristics, the qualities, of someone or something.

You have two writing traits to focus on in this assignment: 1. voice; 2. conventions.

Way back in **Unit 4**, you learned about voice: the true sound of you coming through the writing. But instead of a strong persuasive voice as in your business letter, your voice must sound like an announcer who is observing an event.

Conventions are the rules of writing, like spelling, punctuation, capitalization, and grammar. You will focus on the convention of proper sentences -- that is, *no darn run-ons allowed!!!*

HELPFUL DRILLS

Unlike the memory paper that used the past tense verbs, an observation paper requires the writer to use present tense verbs. All present tense verb forms are spelled the same, except for the third person singular, which always end in *s*.

Examples:

Singular	**Plural**
I walk	we walk
you walk	you (guys) walk
he, she, it *walks*	they walk

The following sentences all contain verbs written in the present tense.

1. The little child picks the apple off the lowest branch.
2. Little Jessica and Ginger jump the rope with blinding speed.
3. Stacey runs to the creek and dives in.
4. Cousin Jerome slurps the chocolate milk shake with gusto.
5. They sing loudly, clap their hands, and stamp their feet.

EXERCISE 10: Read the following passages aloud. Ask yourself, "Am I remembering this?" or "Am I there, watching this happen right now?" If you are remembering this, the action is over and done with. Therefore, it is written in the past tense. If you are there, the action is happening now. It is written in the present tense.

1. The sleeper tosses and turns restlessly. He pulls the blanket up over his head and buries his head in the feather pillow. He dreams that he is drowning. He wakes up and makes a raid on the refrigerator.

2. The sleeper tossed and turned restlessly. He pulled the blanket up over his head and buried his face in the feather pillow. He dreamed that he was drowning. He woke up and made a raid on the refrigerator.

3. The kids stamped their feet. They clapped wildly. They threw confetti. They sang their school song.

4. The kids stamp their feet. They clap wildly. They throw confetti. They sing their school song.

127

EXERCISE 11: Practice changing past tense verbs to present tense verbs in both singular and plural forms. Make sure that singular verbs agree with singular subjects. Remember to add *s* to all verbs that must agree with third person singular subjects (he, she, it).

	Doer	Did (Past Tense)	Do/Does (Present Tense)
1.	They	bought	buy
2.	She	hopped	hops
3.	The rock	smashed	
4.	You and he	hid	
5.	Sammy	heard	
6.	The old saber	hung	
7.	You, Jim,	gave	
8.	We	raised	
9.	The cat	tore	
10.	I	saw	
11.	You girls	flew	
12.	The stallion	ran	
13.	The cow	drank	
14.	A ballerina	spoke	
15.	Glenda and Buzz	whistled	
16.	You	zipped	
17.	The Joneses	took	
18.	We	began	
19.	I	wore	
20.	They	rode	
21.	Patty and I	sat	
22.	Men, you	knew	
23.	The tigress	went	
24.	It	grew	
25.	Aggie	spent	
26.	The bugle	sounded	
27.	He	found	
28.	The Blue Demons	played	
29.	The coach	helped	
30.	Roger and you	fried	

EXERCISE 12: Be sure to recognize present and past helping verbs.

Example: Mai **is walking** quickly.   Present tense = is, are
                     Mai **was walking** quickly.   Past tense = was, were

Tell which sentences are present tense or past tense.

1. Mister Twister was trying to watch the wrestling match.
2. Wait!! A peculiar man is leaping to the stage!
3. The crowd was screaming for a touchdown.
4. Just now the police were called to arrest her.
5. The thousands of fans are finally settling into their seats after an hour delay
   due to the weather.

Before you move on, let's take a moment to rethink the information you learned
from the memory paper and from these most recent exercises. Some short passages follow.
Some use the memory past tense, and some use the observation present tense.

EXERCISE 13: Tell whether the passage is memory past tense or observation present
tense.

1. The tiger smashed into the bars and fell on the meat with a wild embrace.

2. The dishes flew through the air and hit against the wall. Little Becky smiled at her
   work.

3. The kite dances through the air then stops. Suddenly, it screams towards the
   ground.

4. Sameen swayed back and forth across the huge window. Her window washer platform,
   which hung 500 feet in the air, softly flapped against the building.

5. Teresa stands steadily. Her eyes stay on the cobra's weaving head. With the palm
   turned down, her right hand gropes behind her on the table for her pistol.

6. Ruben lifts the lid to inspect the crate. His cat, Mercurio, purrs contentedly beside
   him.

EXERCISE 14: Now look back to **The Terrified Skier** model on page 125.
Reread it and answer the questions on the analysis sheet that follows on a separate
piece of paper. These questions will help you zero in on ways to improve your own
observation paper that you are going to write.

Name_____Date_____

The Terrified Skier Analysis Sheet

1. What is the central action being observed?
2. Who are the Doers in this paper?
3. Where does the action take place?
4. Use the special chart below to list all the actions in the beginning, the middle, and the ending. Use *B*, *M*, or *E* beside the number of the sentence which begins each section of the paper.

Subject (Doer)	**Verb (Do/Does)**	**Number of Words**
Hedy Heinz	*pauses*	*12*

1.
2.
3.
4.
5.
6.
7.
8.
9.
10.
11.
12.
13.
14.
15.
16.
17.
18.

5. Select colorful words from the story that could be added to your word storage bank.

6. The student-writer used several sentence writing skills to improve sentence variety and make her story more interesting. See if you can find the sentences, listing their numbers:
    a. Sentences in which Hedy is the Doer
    b. Sentences in which the bear is the Doer
    c. A sentence in which her heart is the Doer
    d. A sentence in which ice and rocks are the Doers
    e. A sentence which begins with a **glue word**
    f. Sentences which begin with **ING words**

WRITING PROMPT

You are going to write an observation paper. You are reporting the activities of another person. Therefore, instead of using the first person singular pronoun, **I**, that you used in the memory paper, you will be using the third person pronouns.

Imagine that you are in a large stadium, auditorium, theater, or television studio observing one of the following events:

    a   wedding
    b.   athletic contest
    c.   circus
    d.   drama (play) or movie
    e.   ballet, opera, or concert
    f.   a dance contest
    g.   talk show (television)
    h.   graduation ceremony
    i.   political rally or debate
    j.   boxing match
    k.   **your own topic**

During the event, an interloper rushes into the action. You, as an observer, must describe the activities of the intruder.

Your observation must extend from the time the interloper enters the scene until she/he/it is removed by the security force or ushers, or how ever you decide to end this observation.

What you observe will be limited to a brief time and the description of a few, memorable, outstanding actions. Focus on the actions of the intruder, not on the reactions of others.

YOUR ATTENTION PLEASE

You may be tempted to write your observation from your point of view, such as "I am sitting in the rock concert, and suddenly I notice a person jumping onto the stage."

Remember that you do not need to write using *I*. You should write, "All the seats are full at the rock concert. The fans are loving this excellent performance. Just now a person jumps onto the stage . . . "

ORGANIZING YOUR IDEAS

Plunge immediately into the action. Do not worry about setting the scene or padding your paper with unnecessary background information.

Begin with the interloper's first action. Then, report on all the subsequent actions from the beginning to the end of the incident. Think of specific details of what the interloper did at each stage of the observed incident. Use your imagination. Stretch it!

To help you in your effort, at this point the class will select one of the suggested topics and work through it as a class project. Your teacher can jot down your ideas on the blackboard or an overhead projector transparency. When it comes time to write your paper, you **cannot** use the same topic which the class chose for its practice project.

In case you do not want to use one of the suggested topics for this class project, the following can serve as an introduction to your class composed observation paper.

> The candidate for mayor, Dr. N.O.S. Bleed, wipes her forehead and continues to speak. Suddenly the audience's attention is directed to an interloper, dressed in shocking pink body tights, who rushes to the speaker's platform.

Observation Paper Think Sheet

Purpose: You will describe the intruder's moments *in the spotlight*. Before you begin to write your first draft, fill out the following **Think Sheet**. It will help you to know your subject better.

1.   Where and when does the incident take place?

2.   What voice will you be using? **Trait 1?**

3.   What type of event is taking place?

4.   Who is the interloper?

5.   What does the intruder look like? Use colorful and descriptive words. Is the interloper carrying anything?

6.   With what activity does the interloper burst onto the scene?

7.   List the intruder's actions you observed from the beginning to the end. List specific details with each action. Stretch it! Remember to use the journalistic questions to stimulate your thoughts.

     Events   **Specific Details**
    a.

    b.

    c.

    d.

    e.

    f.

    g.

    h.

    i.

8.   What three ways do you know to avoid those ruinous run-ons--trait 2?

9.   What *new* word can you invent for this paper?

STAGE TWO: WRITING THE FIRST DRAFT

When you finish your **Think Sheet**, begin writing your first draft. Be sure to number each of your sentences and to skip lines, as always.

Here are some other things which you should try to do as you write your paper:

1. Limit the time and space in which your observation takes place.
2. Plunge directly into the action as you begin writing.
3. Move from the beginning to the end. Add specific details with each event. If you cannot think of specific details, ask yourself the questions **who, what, when, where, why,** and **how.**
4. Use third person pronouns. Do not use *I.*
5. Always use present tense (do/does) verbs.
6. Try to begin your sentences with different openings.
7. Try to add a new word you invented for this paper.

Sentence Opening Sheet (SOS) Help Sheet

Once your first draft is finished, it is time to fill out a **Sentence Opening Sheet.** Fill out each column according to the following set of instructions.

Column 1: Sentence Openings

Write down the first four words of each sentence.
  a. Do any of your sentences begin with interesting patterns? (Example: **glue words** or **ING words**?)
  b. Do you repeat the name of the central character over and over again?
  c. Do you repeat the same third person pronoun over and over again?

Column 2: Special--Doer

Is the Doer always the third person singular or plural?

Column 3: Verbs (DO/DOES words)

List all the verbs in each sentence.
  a. Are all the verbs in present tense?
  b. Do all the verbs agree in number with the subject?

Column 4: Number of Words Per Sentence

List the number of words in each sentence.
  a. Do any of the shorter sentences need to be combined to make the sentence patterns more interesting?
  b. Do the longer sentences have proper *gluing*, or are they run-ons?

Sentence Opening Sheet

Name

First Four Words Per Sentence	Special	Verbs	# of Words

STAGE THREE: REWRITING

Before you write your final draft, you will be proofreading a partner's paper as you did with the **Memory Paper**. The following student model contains typical errors you will want to look for when it's time for your proofreading.

Big Trouble

1. As the bell clangs, Phil Erup roars out of the classroom. **2.** By the time he nears the corner of the hall, he moved in a blur of motion. **3.** Mrs. Trombone, the music teacher, hums to herself as she approaches the same corner from the other direction. **4.** They click down the hallway as she thinks about her coffee break. **5.** His sneakers pound the tiles as he was rushing to be the first in the lunch line. **6.** The chowhound turned the corner at full speed and slams into Mrs. Trombone. **7.** His breath comes in short gasps while he looks up from the floor. **8.** With one eye he sees a *Don't run in the hall* sign. **9.** With the other, he saw a smiling Mrs. Trombone who weigh 98 pounds.

1. In which sentences has the writer switched from present to past tense?
2. In which sentence has the writer switched to a plural pronoun, making the sentence sound confusing? Correct it.
3. In which sentence is the subject in some form of the third person singular pronoun?
4. In which sentence is the wrong form of the present tense verb used?

Before you write your final draft, trade papers with your partner. Use the **Checklist Sheet** as your guide. Correct any spelling errors you are able to spot. Also, check for fragments and run-ons. The errors you find in your partner's paper could be and may be similar to your own. That's why it's so important to go over your partner's paper with a fine-tooth comb.

Observation Paper Checklist

1. What is the action being observed? Whose voice do you hear (**trait 1**)?

2. How much time passes?

3. Where does the incident take place? When?

4. If the beginning, middle, and ending are not clear and interesting, give some specific suggestions to the writer about how the observation paper can be corrected. Applying the journalistic questions to each action of the interloper will give you some ideas for coloring-up the reporting of the incident.

5. Are all the writer's verbs in the present tense? If they are not, record the sentence numbers that have past tense verbs.

6. Is the subject of each sentence, the Doer, in the same form of the third person singular or plural?

7. Are all the pronouns the writer uses in the third person singular or plural? If not, record the sentence numbers that do not have third person pronouns.

8. Check to see that the sentence openings are not all the same. Suggest specific ways to make the sentence openings more interesting and varied on the first draft.

9. Do you see any spelling errors? Circle them on the first draft.

10. Help your partner correct all fragments and run-ons (**trait 2**) you find.

11. What is the new word your partner *authored*?

STAGE FOUR: PUBLISHING

Since you will be sharing your story with an audience, you need to clean it up. Recopy it neatly onto a fresh sheet of paper making sure that spelling, punctuation, and capitalization are in A-1 order.

Your observation paper reveals the action of an event as it happens. To capture this live report, pretend you are a news reporter for either a TV or radio station. Read your report into a tape recorder or in front of a video camera. Then play it back to your class.

Oral Language into Writing

FLEXIBLE WORDS

As you recognized in **Unit 2,** the order of words can change the meaning of sentences. Do you remember Mario, the greedy, foolish grape-eater on page 33? What was Mario's dilemma? In an interesting way, you learned that word order is very flexible.

Flexible word order can change not only the position of a word but the meaning and the use of the word. Our language allows us to play with word order to change the meaning of a sentence.

Notice the difference in meaning of these two sentences which use the same three words.

1. Rodney flies airships.
2. Rodney airships flies.

Can you explain what Rodney does in both jobs?

1. As a pilot for the Goodyear Rubber Corporation, Rodney flies blimps (airships).

2. To keep him company on long trips, Rodney takes his pet insects with him. In other words, he airships flies!

WARM-UP ACTIVITY 1

Explain Rodney's job in each of the examples. Then, flip-flop the second and third words, and explain Rodney's new job. This warm-up might be completed as a cooperative learning activity.

1. Rodney bags paints.
   Rodney_____

2. Rodney cuts dresses.
   Rodney _____

3. Rodney shovels walks.
   Rodney_____

4. Rodney guards fences.
Rodney_____

5. Rodney marks trails.
Rodney_____

6. Rodney boxes soaps.
Rodney_____

7. Rodney locks drawers.
Rodney_____

8. Rodney snaps covers.
Rodney_____

WARM-UP ACTIVITY 2

Select your two favorite, flip-flopped jobs from **WARM-UP ACTIVITY 1**. Write a paragraph about Rodney's change of employment which answers these questions.

   1. Where did Rodney work?
   2. What did he do on that job? (Supply details)
   3. Why did he change jobs?
   4. What does he do in his new job? (Supply details)

As in the model paragraph **The Big Blizzard**, underline Rodney's old and new jobs in your paragraph. Number each sentence, too.

The Big Blizzard

1. While working in the hardware department of Sneers, Robot, and Co., Rodney sold many kinds of tools to his customers. **2.** Rakes were very popular in the fall until the weather became colder, and a wicked storm blew into town. **3.** After twenty-six inches of snow had fallen, customers trudged over to Sneers to buy shovels. **4.** Because the snow was so deep, poor Rodney had to <u>walk the shovels</u> from the hardware department to the customers' cars in the parking lot. **5.** Rodney tripped twice, soaked his Reeboks, and was snowballed by some mischievous kids. **6.** The cold made his fingers turn blue. **7.** The next day he quit to take a new job <u>covering snaps</u> in the notions department.

140

REARRANGING

The skills which you have learned so far in *Open the Deck* are important and useful for everyday writing. **Combining** and **expanding** are the important skills you **have learned**. Now that you are writing more, you may find yourself wanting to change sentences around for variety to create impact. To do this, you would need to **rearrange**.

For example, look at this sentence.

> When the game was in its closing moments, Scott John slipped around the goalie and scored the winning goal.

If the writer wanted to experiment, she could rewrite this sentence in the following ways:

> Scott John scored the winning goal as he slipped around the goalie in the closing moments of the game.
>
> **or**
>
> Slipping around the goalie in the closing moments of the game, Scott John scored the winning goal.

This re-shuffling action is easy and fun. Discuss the variety created.

EXERCISE 1: **Rearrange** the following sentences. Form at least one new sentence which has the same meaning as the original one.

1. Yelling at the baby-sitter, Jennifer flipped her strained spinach onto the floor.

2. Clem Periwinkle ate creamed catfish for dinner last night.

3. The multi-colored balloon lurched wildly as it climbed into the sky.

4. It gave the beauty queen lockjaw to smile at everybody all the time.

5. Georgio, the singing Slovak baker, makes cream pies and hot cross buns.

6. Jumping into the huge vat of Jell-O, Norman stubbed his toe.

7. Little Lester walked cautiously into the haunted house on a stormy night.

8. When the roast pig is finished, immediately stick an apple in its mouth.

9. Working at home, Shawna made twenty dozen chocolate chip cookies in the stove.

10. "Get it yourself, ape man," screamed Cheetah angrily.

COMBINING AND REARRANGING

Rearrange is your third writer's vocabulary word. Now that you can manipulate sentences with this skill, let's see if you can move one step further. See if you can **combine** sentences and then **rearrange** them to add variety. With every accomplishment, you are becoming more skillful with the language you use.

To get started, study these sentences:

> The tuba player played loudly.
> The tuba player was wacky.
> The tuba player played in the bathtub.

Here are at least three possible ways these sentences could be **combined** and then **rearranged**:

Examples:

1. The wacky tuba player played loudly in the bathtub.
2. In the bathtub the wacky tuba player played loudly.
3. The tuba player, who was wacky, played loudly in the bathtub.

EXERCISE 2: **Combine** and **rearrange** the following sentence sets. Write two different sentences for each set. Your second sentence should begin with a different opening than the first one. In other words, we want variety.

1. The spaceship was blinking its lights.
   The spaceship was enormous.
   The spaceship was receiving a speeding ticket.

2. The octopus was green.
   The octopus played the accordion.
   The octopus strolled through the waves.

3. The marshmallow was toasted.
   The marshmallow was toasted carefully.
   The marshmallow was melted onto the chocolate square.

4. The car had been purchased.
   The car had been purchased by a millionaire.
   The car was painted gold.
   The millionaire was a basketball player.

5. Seymour roller-skated to school.
   Seymour roller-skated through the rain.
   Seymour roller-skated in the morning.
   Seymour roller-skated four miles.

6. The football players practiced in the cold.
The football players practiced twice a day.
The football players practiced in new uniforms.
The football players were excited.

7. The monkey searched for fleas.
The monkey was cute.
The monkey swung towards the people.
The people were smiling.

8. The player slam-dunked the ball.
The player was short.
The player let out a whoop.
The player was hot-dogging.

ANOTHER WRITER'S VOCABULARY PRACTICE

As you have been working, you probably have thought of many ways some sentences could be rearranged. Here's another chance to **combine** sentences and then **rearrange** them in two sentence patterns.

For example, here are the original sentences:

Old: The vulture sits in the tree. The vulture just became hungry.

New: The vulture, which just became hungry, sits in the tree.

or

Sitting in the tree, the vulture just became hungry.

or

In the tree sits the vulture which just became hungry.

Of the three revised sentences, which one do you like best? Why? Defend your choice.

EXERCISE 3: Now, you try it on your own. Follow the examples above.

1. The cockroach is hiding under the plate.
The cockroach just escaped from Raid.

2. Horatio just ate three large gyros sandwiches.
Horatio looked awful.

143

3 . Bubba is a great running back.
Bubba goes to Whispering Pines High School.

4 . The volcano was angry.
The volcano spouted for days.

5 . It was Thursday.
The pansies sprouted.
The pansies sprouted in the garden.

6 . The mud was slimy.
Tommy Butz squished through the mud.
Tommy Butz slipped and fell.

7 . Roberta powdered her nose.
Roberta powdered her nose in the dim light.
Roberta's nose was sunburned.

8 . The tumbleweed rolled down the hill.
The tumbleweed was large and fat.
The tumbleweed rolled into the well.
The well was dark.

9 . The water was foamy.
Britt rafted through the water.
Britt was tipped into the raging current.

1 0 . We picked huckleberries.
We sorted them.
We sold them to the bears.
The bears were happy.

MINI-REVIEW OF YOUR WRITER'S VOCABULARY

Remember your **writer's vocabulary** as you are writing and revising your composition. Here's a quick review:

> **Combine** sentences to add variety to your sentence openings and structures.

> **Expand** with specific details to support your ideas.

> **Rearrange** sentence parts to create impact upon your audience.

Major Writing Assignment

EXPLAINING WHAT YOU KNOW

In almost any career you choose, you will sometimes be expected to explain something to someone else in writing. This might include giving directions (as in a memo to other workers), describing a new product to clients, explaining why you are doing something, or writing up an idea you have for your own boss.

Even now in school you are expected to be able to write about what you have learned in other subjects. In this writing assignment you will receive some practice which you can use in science or social studies or math--not just English.

All the sentence writing skills you have been learning so far will help make it easier for you to do this kind of *talking* on paper. This type of writing is also known as **expository writing**.

STAGE ONE: PREWRITING

STUDENT LEARNING OBJECTIVES

1. The student will explain something she knows.
2. The student will organize her information in a logical order.
3. The student will write a catchy opening to arouse her audience's interest.
4. The student will support her ideas with specific examples.
5. The student will stretch some of her sentences to make them more informative and interesting.
6. The student will combine some sentences so that they have different lengths and patterns.

WHERE DO I START?

The most important choice you are going to have for this assignment is selecting a topic. You will remember from **Unit 5** that the trait of **ideas** is one of the most important for you to master as you develop writing skills. In this paper, the topic can come from any class you have: history, math, science, physical education, foreign language, home economics, health. Your own interests outside of school are also fair game--especially if they somehow relate to something you have been studying in school.

Since you are going to spend time brainstorming this topic, you should select one that interests you and that you would enjoy writing about. Your purpose is to inform and get your audience as excited and as interested in the topic as you are. You may even find yourself gathering more information about the topic as you go along.

SAMPLE THINK SHEET

Elva has completed her own think sheet to show what she knows about her topic. Read through her think sheet to see how she collected her information.

Name _____ Elva Ramirez _____ **Date** _____ Feb. 13 _____

Topic of Interest _____ Harriet Tubman, "The Moses of Her People" _____

1. What I Know:

a. Harriet Tubman was born a slave but gained her freedom and helped more than 800 slaves escape to the North before the Civil War.

b. It is said that Harriet was one of the most remarkable African American woman who ever lived in this country.

c. Harriet lived to be almost a hundred years old, and before she died she had many exciting adventures.

d. My friend Darnelle's mother says that Harriet Tubman was braver than you can possibly imagine.

3. Where I Looked:

Golden Legacy, illustrated history
    magazine
Talked to Dr. Bob Sagor, a Civil War history
    buff
Talked to my friend's mom who is a college
    teacher
Read some articles our teacher had us
    read for social studies
Read two books suggested by the librarian
Check the Internet

2. What I Want to Know:

a. What were the most interesting and unusual parts of Harriet's life?

b. How did Harriet gain her own freedom?

c. What were the tricks Harriet used to help the other slaves escape?

d. What are some examples of the scary, but brave things that Harriet did?

e. How could I find out more about Harriet?

4. What I Discovered:

a. When Harriet Tubman was fourteen years old, she tried to help a young slave who was about to be beaten. She stood between the man with the whip (the overseer) and the slave, and she was hit in the head with a rock by the overseer.

b. This wound almost killed Harriet but she lived. However, this injury hurt Harriet for the rest of her life. From time to time, she would suddenly fall into a deep sleep from which no one could wake her.

c. When Harriet's original master died, she escaped all by herself. She didn't want to be sold. More importantly, she did not want to be a slave any longer.

d. During her escape, Harriet traveled only at night, and she used the north star as a guide. She also knew that moss grew on the north side of trees so that helped her.

e. Harriet traveled all the way to Philadelphia, two hundred miles on foot.

f. Once she was free, Harriet saved money and returned to the south over and over again to help other slaves flee to the North.

g. These groups of slaves had to cross many rivers and only travel at night. Along the way anti-slavery groups helped the slaves and Harriet hide in safe stations. This trail to freedom became known as the Underground Railroad.

h. Once during a really dangerous trip Harriet's old injury acted up and she fell into a deep sleep. Unlike most times, however, she woke up quickly and was able to lead the group to safety.

i. Harriet helped some slaves escape more than once, and she even broke them out of jail.

j. After helping more than 800 slaves find freedom, Harriet became a nurse and military scout for the Union Army during the Civil War. She went behind enemy lines many times but escaped without injury.

k. Harriet lived for almost fifty years after the Civil War and died in 1913.

THINKING ABOUT THE SAMPLE THINK SHEET

As you read through the **GETTING STARTED INVENTORY THINK SHEET**, you will notice that Elva first had to write down all the information she already knew about Harriet Tubman. Since she had just studied this topic in social studies, she was able to get some information from her class readings and also from her class notes. She listed all this information under the section marked, **WHAT I KNOW**.

Under the section **WHAT I WANT TO KNOW**, Elva listed many questions after listening to her friend's mom. Her curiosity had grown because her friend's mother, a college teacher, made Harriet Tubman sound like a remarkable woman. Most of these questions came right from Elva's own curiosity. These questions then guided her to search for some new sources. Notice that she listed these new sources under the **WHERE I LOOKED** section.

Finally, Elva listed all the new information she found under the **WHAT I DISCOVERED** section. These pieces of information helped her write a complete explanation about Harriet Tubman. Elva was able to combine what she already knew and what she discovered.

SELECTING A TOPIC

Now that you have studied Elva's **Think Sheet**, it is time for you to select a topic to write about. Remember, the topic should be interesting to you. Your purpose is to inform your audience about this topic, getting them as excited as you are.

Here are some topics other students have decided to use for this assignment. They are only listed here to give you some ideas.

Sample Topics

  A. Explain the most important points of an interesting article you have read.
  B. Compare and contrast the habitats of two animals.
  C. Explain how to find some special piece of information in the library.
  D. Explain why knowledge of nutrition is a necessity for a healthy life.
  E. Explain some of the most interesting facts about a famous mathematician.

Brainstorm a list of three possible topics, like the ones above, and then conference with your teacher to settle on a final selection.

Once you've done this, then you're ready to get to work on your own **GETTING STARTED INVENTORY THINK SHEET**.

COMPLETING YOUR OWN THINK SHEET

Now that you have a topic to work with, fill out your own **GETTING STARTED INVENTORY THINK SHEET**. Remember that Elva had to use a lot more space on her own inventory. That's normal. Use as much room as you need to cover the topic.

Your **Think Sheet** should contain all the information you will need to inform and interest your reader. This type of writing is called expository writing because its purpose is to explain.

Now begin working on your **Think Sheet**.

GETTING STARTED INVENTORY THINK SHEET

Name _____Date _____

Topic of Interest: _____

1. What I Know:	2. What I Want to Know:

3. Where I Looked:

4. What I Discovered:

HELPFUL DRILL 1--SUPPORTING STATEMENTS

Soon you are going to use your own **Think Sheet** to write your own expository assignment. First, however, these helpful drills will make it a little easier to best use the information you have.

In your own expository writing, you must elaborate your major points with supporting statements. These examples or extra information help the reader to fully understand what you are trying to say.

Let's practice how to include this necessary information in practice statements below before you start writing your first draft. Work orally with your teacher and class by providing supporting statements or further explanations. Use the **GETTING STARTED INVENTORY THINK SHEET** which the student Elva wrote as a source for your information or use your own knowledge about Harriet Tubman.

For each practice statement, try to compose one or two supporting sentences. Some students will share these on the board. Read the sample first.

Sample:

> *General Statement*
>
> Harriet Tubman had to overcome many problems in order to achieve her goals.
>
> *Supporting Facts*
>
> 1. For example, she had a life-long injury which caused her to become unconscious sometimes, even during dangerous escapes.
>
> 2. Also, Harriet had to travel on some of her most dangerous journeys on her own with no one to help her.
>
> 3. Harriet had to work continually to raise money to help fund her efforts.

Now try to write your own supporting statements for the practice statements.

1. Harriet Tubman accomplished many things in her life which were remarkable.

2. Escaping slaves did many things to try to increase their chances of making it to the North before being caught.

3. Life as a slave was often cruel and harsh.

HELPFUL DRILL 2--CATCHY OPENING

In any type of expository paper, it's usually important to define your topic very clearly. Remember that you are explaining. Again using Elva's topic, decide which of the following examples is the best beginning paragraph.

Example A

> Have you heard about a woman named Harriet Tubman? She was brave and lived a long time ago. I think she lived before the Civil War. Once she was a slave. When she wasn't any more she did some neat things. The Underground Railroad was one. Slavery was very cruel. Harriet helped some people escape. She helped about 800 of them.

Example B

> Harriet Tubman was a wonderful, African American woman. Her exciting life began in slavery and took her to a path of fame and the role of a heroine. Her life was more adventurous and interesting than almost any make-believe character you ever read about in a book.

Example C

> Harriet Tubman was a wonderful woman and American. Her adventurous life began in slavery and took her on a path to fame and the role of a heroine. Most of all, Harriet is remembered as the African American woman who helped more than 800 slaves escape to freedom before the Civil War. As a slave her life was very hard and she was often beaten. She became seriously hurt when she tried to help a slave escape. This was because she was hit on the head with a brick. In this paper you'll see why Harriet Tubman is exciting. I will cover many things in this paper.

1. Which example do you think best sets up the discussion of one main idea and helps to lead into the rest of the paper?

2. What problems do the other two examples have?

3. What things does the best paragraph do to help lead into the second paragraph? How does it help to make the reader want to keep reading?

WRITING YOUR OWN INTRODUCTION

Write an opening paragraph for your short paper. Be sure to set up the one main idea you will be discussing. Try to set the stage for the reader, but don't include all your ideas and information in the first paragraph.

STAGE TWO: WRITING THE FIRST DRAFT

Now it's time to write your own paper using the good introduction you have already written.

Here are some important ground rules for you as you get ready to write.

- Write something which you think will be interesting for others to read. Would you want to read this yourself?

- Get into your main topic right at the beginning.

- Write about one main idea in each paragraph-- do not jam all your information in one *loooong* paragraph.

- Try to support all your key statements with at least one example. Two is even better.

- Organize your major points in a logical sequence.

- Vary your sentence lengths.

- **Expand** and **combine** sentences.

STAGE THREE: REWRITING

When your first draft is finished, you'll want to check it over and make improvements. Use the editor's **Checklist Sheet**. Notice that you will be working with an editing partner.

INFORMING CHECKLIST

1. What is the topic of this assignment?

2. Does the writer use some good examples to help show her main ideas? Please list a few here.

3. Are the major points organized in a logical sequence?

4. What is *best* about this paper?

5. What one thing could the writer do to improve this paper?

6. Please number each sentence. Which sentences (list numbers) are ones which have been expanded well?

7. What words are misspelled? Circle them.

8. Put a box around any vocabulary words which you think work well in this paper.

9. List any sentence numbers which have punctuation errors.

STAGE FOUR: PUBLISHING

Write a final draft of your paper using your very best handwriting. Attach your paper to a small poster which uses some type of illustration or pictures to describe your topic. These posters will be displayed in the classroom. Way to show what you know!

STAGE ONE: PREWRITING

STUDENT LEARNING OBJECTIVES

1. The student will write a report about a famous person, including specific information about the individual's life.
2. The student will organize his/her famous person report according to the format given, including an introduction, at least five body paragraphs (each one telling something different about the famous person), and a conclusion.
3. The student's writing will have sentence fluency by using sentence combining skills to convert notes into sentences.
4. The student will write a bibliography listing the sources of information.
5. The student will include a drawing, an illustration, or a photograph of the famous person.
6. The student will use correct conventions: punctuate correctly, capitalize the correct words, and avoid fragments and run-ons.
7. The student's report will have a cover.

WRITING PROMPT

Your last assignment is to write a paper about a famous person. Your paper will give facts, or true statements, about this person. The purpose is to inform the audience. This type of writing is called an expository report.

ORGANIZING YOUR IDEAS

Your report will need an introduction and a conclusion. It will also have at least five body paragraphs, each one telling something interesting about the famous person. Paragraphs could be about the person's childhood, family, education, motivation, hardships, and achievements.

In addition, the report will include a cover which projects and brightens it. The report will also include a bibliography listing the sources of information. Finally, you will need an illustration that can be a drawing, tracing, or photograph showing what the famous person looks like. If you borrow or copy the illustration from somewhere rather than creating it yourself, be sure to include a citation beneath it to give credit where credit is due.

CHOICE OF A TOPIC

What famous person are you interested in reporting on? Your choice can be an individual you are studying in one of your other classes. What about a historical figure? A scientist? Your favorite author? Your hero?

Here is a list of types of famous persons to help you decide. Pick a second person, too, in case someone else selects your first choice. Also, maybe enough information cannot be found about your first choice. Remember, some well-known people recently became famous, and not much has been written about them yet.

U.S. presidents	scientists
Canadian Prime Ministers	inventors
historical figures, like early explorers	authors
sports stars: football, soccer, etc.	
entertainers/movie stars	
consider people of color, like famous Asian Americans, Mexican Americans, African Americans, Native Americans	
your choice	

SOURCES: PLACES TO LOOK

So you don't know enough about the famous person to write five paragraphs? You're not sure if some information is fact or just a rumor? You are very interested in your famous person, and you want to learn more about the person?

Sources are persons, books, or places that supply information. Since you need to gather information about your famous person topic, sources will be used.

Books about your famous person in the library or your classroom are good sources. **Encyclopedias** have information for you, too. **Newspaper** and **magazine** articles also supply information. If you have access to the **Internet**, try searching the World Wide Web or some other on-line resource.

There may be someone who is an expert on your famous person who could be very helpful. Maybe a movie, filmstrip, or television show you know about has information about your topic. Perhaps you can write a business letter to the famous person's television network, recording studio, or professional team to gather information.

Your teacher or media specialist/ librarian will help you find sources.

Remember, you must be able to locate at least two sources about your topic choice in order to practice finding enough information to write an interesting report.

BIBLIOGRAPHY INFORMATION: GIVE CREDIT TO BORROWED NOTES

Because you are using someone else's book or article, you must give the author credit.

Here are some examples of a bibliography on a report about Dr. Martin Luther King, Jr.:

If the information comes from an encyclopedia:

> "Martin Luther King, Jr.," *Collier's Encyclopedia*, 1990 edition, volume 14, page 90.

If the information comes from a book, use this model:

> *Martin Luther King, Jr.*, by Jacqueline L. Harris, Franklin Watts Company, New York, 1983.
>
> or
>
> *Martin Luther King, Jr. Free at Last*, by David A. Alder, Holiday House, New York, 1986.

If the information comes from an Internet web site:

> Martin Luther King Day Web page. Seattle Times. 12 January 1999 <http://www.seatimes.com>

NOTE-TAKING: WRITE IT DOWN

After you have found sources you need for this report, it's time to really get started with your research. Begin by asking yourself questions. For example, one question might be *What do I want to know about this person?* Organize these questions into categories, i. e., education, lifestyle, childhood, jobs held, hardships, motivation, etc.

Do not trust your memory alone. Write down on paper the information you learn. This is called taking notes. Notes are short phrases. Do not worry about fragments; they are all right for now. Be careful to include enough information with **glue words** to be able to understand your notes.

Use your own words instead of copying the texts of your sources. Younger students tend to believe that writing a report means opening a book or encyclopedia and copying a couple of paragraphs. This is not writing. It is known as **plagiarism**--stealing someone's ideas and work.

Rather than copying, you will paraphrase. In other words, choose different words that convey the same ideas. This will help you understand the information. Also, your own words will be easier to use when you put the information into paragraphs for your report.

Notes on Dr. Martin Luther King, Jr.

Suppose someone has chosen Dr. Martin Luther King, Jr. for a famous person report topic. Maybe the writer is interested in finding out more about this man, famed as a civil rights leader.

Looking in the encyclopedia and books mentioned on page 159, the writer took notes, using his own words instead of copying.

1. born in Atlanta, Georgia

2. born in 1929

3. lived under Jim Crow laws

4. blacks were kept in separate schools

5. blacks and whites had different restaurants, hotels, neighborhoods

6. his dad was pastor of a church

7. mother was a teacher

8. had one brother and one sister

9. his grandfather had been a slave before the Civil War

10. Martin experienced prejudice

11. strategy of civil disobedience

12. first job was minister of Baptist church in Montgomery, Alabama

13. Rosa Parks arrested in 1955--refused to sit in back of bus

14. MLK led boycott of buses as a protest

15. they won because Supreme Court ruled it was illegal to segregate on public buses

16. he was jailed many times for protest

17. wrote famous letter about his beliefs from a Birmingham jail in '63

18. *I Have a Dream* speech in Washington, D.C., in 1963

19. 250,000 people marched there for jobs and freedom

20. woman stabbed him in New York, but he lived

21. used sit-ins as nonviolent protest

22. used *freedom rides*--they'd drive to different towns that were segregated and then sit in for equal rights

23. studied ideas of Mahatma Gandhi

24. Gandhi opposed British rule of his India

25. used nonviolence to change unfair laws

HELPFUL DRILL: NOTE-TAKING PRACTICE

Let's pretend you selected Amelia Earhart for your famous person report topic. Read the selection and take five notes as you read. Use your own words. Paraphrase. Do not plagiarize!

Born in Atchison, Kansas, in 1897, Amelia Earhart nursed wounded soldiers during World War I. After the war, her interest in becoming a pilot led her to California where she earned money for flying lessons.

In 1928, Miss Earhart became the first female passenger on a transatlantic flight, flying from Newfoundland to Burry Port, Wales. Four years later she flew across the Atlantic alone. Later she was the first woman to fly from Honolulu to the United States mainland. She also flew across the United States alone in both directions.

During an attempt to fly around the world, she lost her life. Her plane vanished at sea.

Taking Notes

1. _____

2. _____

3. _____

4. _____

5. _____

HELPFUL DRILL: ORGANIZING THE NOTES

Now we return to the famous civil rights leader, Dr. Martin Luther King, Jr. On page 161 there are twenty-five notes about him. These notes must be organized into groups or categories to make paragraphs.

After reading and rereading all twenty-five notes, the student-writer first grouped them as follows:

1.	Early Years	1, 2, 6, 7, 8
2.	Prejudice	3, 4, 5, 9,10
3.	Civil disobedience	11, 16
4.	Rosa Parks	13, 14, 15
5.	Famous speech	18, 19
6.	Nonviolent protest	21, 22
7.	Influence of Gandhi	23, 24, 25

She then further sorted these seven into five in the interest of organizing her paper better. This is how they were reclassified.

1.	Early Years	1, 2, 6, 7, 8
2.	Prejudice	3, 4, 5, 9, 10
3.	Civil disobedience	11, 13, 14, 15, 16, 21, 22
4.	Famous speech	18, 19
5.	Influence of Gandhi	23, 24, 25

Try to explain why the notes were grouped under each topic. Do you agree with the writer's choices? Notice that 12, 17, and 20 were left out. Since they did not fit into any group, they were dropped. However, if as many as five or six notes didn't fit into groups, then maybe the categories should be changed or more notes added to the report.

When you begin to take notes and group them into specific categories, make sure you have enough information to write your famous person report. If you do not have enough information, you will have to research more. Then, you can add to your list of notes.

The student who took the Dr. Martin King Jr. notes had to read more than just the encyclopedia article to include additional information. Remember: The assignment calls for at least five paragraphs in the body of the paper, so you will need to read more than one source.

HELPFUL DRILL: CATEGORIZING NOTES

Leona, a student from Eugene, Oregon, decided to write her report on the famous genius Albert Einstein, the scientist whose investigations changed the study of physics. Below are the notes she took from the book *Albert Einstein*, by Milton Dank, Franklin Watts, New York, 1983.

1. born in Germany on March 14, 1879
2. father gave him a magnetic compass as a gift when he was five years old
3. this was his first interest in science
4. was bored in school
5. Max Talmy, a university student invited to their house, shared physics books with Albert
6. Albert taught himself geometry at home
7. expelled from high school for being unruly and undisciplined
8. moved to Switzerland to go to school at the Federal Institute of Technology
9. courses taught Newtonian physics
10. he studied new ideas on his own
11. married Mileva Maric in 1903
12. she was a science student, too
13. unhappy marriage
14. took a job at the government patent office because he needed money to support his family
15. in 1905 he wrote an article about light opposing Newtonian physics
16. didn't get much attention
17. theory of relativity
18. figured that time passes at different speeds when people are moving
19. scientists didn't understand the importance at first
20. wife not allowed to work with him
21. marriage fell apart
22. relativity theory proved true in 1919
23. met his cousin Elsa again in 1917
24. she took care of him during serious illness
25. had been a childhood friend
26. they married
27. he became famous in 1920
28. photographs of solar eclipse proved deflection of starlight--relativity

After reading and rereading her list of notes, she decided on these five groups:

Group 1   early interests
Group 2   problems in school
Group 3   Newtonian old ideas
Group 4   theory of relativity
Group 5   marriage

EXERCISE 1: Under each main topic that Leona came up with, list the notes from page 164 that belong in that category. Some notes do not fit under any group. Be ready to explain why you grouped the notes the way you did. The first three have been done for you.

Group 1	early interests	2, 3, ___
Group 2	problems in school	
Group 3	Newtonian old ideas	
Group 4	theory of relativity	
Group 5	marriage	
No Group		1, ___

HELPFUL DRILL: COMBINING AND EXPANDING NOTES INTO PARAGRAPHS

A group of notes next becomes sentences that build into a paragraph. Using a pencil, the writer **expanded** the notes into complete ideas with a *Doer* and a *Does*. She **combined** some sentences using **glue words**.

Leona decided to change the order of the notes because she felt it was better organized. Since all the sentences are about the same topic, Leona put them together in a paragraph. Notice that the first sentence tells the audience the topic.

Here is her paragraph about **Group 4**, Einstein's *theory of relativity* using notes 17, 18, 19, 22, and 28.

- **17.** theory of relativity
- **18.** figured that time passes at different speeds when people are moving
- **19.** scientists didn't understand the importance at first
- **22.** relativity theory proved true in 1919
- **28.** photographs of solar eclipse proved deflection of starlight--relativity

Einstein is best known for his (17) theory of relativity which proved

(18) time passes at different speeds for two people when they are

moving. It was (22) proven true in 1919 when (28) photographs of a solar

eclipse proved the deflection of starlight. It is interesting to note that at

first (19) scientists at this time did not even understand the importance of

Einstein's theory.

Notice how Leona used **glue words** to combine her notes into sentences. Name the **WH word** that combines notes 17 and 18. What **glue word** combines note 22 with 28? When a writer smoothly combines ideas (notes) into sentences that flow nicely along, she has met the trait of sentence fluency.

EXERCISE 2: From the notes on Einstein's marriages, write a paragraph using all the notes. Remember:

1. you can change the order,
2. use **glue words** to combine some notes, and
3. begin with a sentence that states the topic of the paragraph (marriage).

THINK SHEET

Here is a **Think Sheet** that should be completed for your famous person report. It will help you gather and organize information so that you can write five paragraphs.

Name_____ Date_____

FAMOUS PERSON REPORT THINK SHEET

Purpose: You will write a famous person report in at least five paragraphs about a famous person of your choice.

1. What person are you reporting on?_____

2. What is your alternate topic?_____

3. List at least two sources that give information about your topic:

    a. _____

    b. _____

4. Take notes from your sources, using your own words instead of copying from the book. Fragments are allowed for note-taking purposes. Your notes should be the answers from your questions.

    a. _____

    b. _____

    c. _____

    d. _____

    e. _____

    f. _____

    g. _____

    h. _____

    i. _____

    j. _____

    k. _____

l. _____

m. _____

n. _____

o. _____

p. _____

q. _____

r. _____

s. _____

t. _____

u. _____

v. _____

w. _____

x. _____

y. _____

z. _____

5. If you have not already done so, organize the source information in the correct bibliographic form. Give credit where credit is due. Models are on page 159. Your bibliographic information should be included on a separate page, the last one in your report.

_____

_____

_____

_____

_____

EXERCISE 2: Before you begin to group your notes into specific categories, your teacher will duplicate some volunteer **Think Sheets**. For practice, see if you can group the various notes into specific categories from which you can build paragraphs.

Now, after completing this exercise in studying your own notes, group your notes under five or six topic headings. If you do not have enough information, you might need to read one or two more articles on your famous person topic.

Name_____ Date_____

FAMOUS PERSON REPORT
CATEGORIZED IDEAS THINK SHEET

Group 1 _____
_____
_____
_____

Group 2 _____
_____
_____
_____

Group 3 _____
_____
_____
_____

Group 4 _____
_____
_____
_____

Group 5 _____
_____
_____
_____

Group 6 _____
_____
_____
_____

STAGE TWO: WRITING THE FIRST DRAFT

Using your **Think Sheet**, write the first draft of your famous person report, skipping every other line and numbering each sentence.

Each group of notes needs to be **expanded** into complete sentences. You may need to ask yourself the journalistic questions.

Combine some sentences, using **glue words**, **ING words**, and **WH words** to build a paragraph for each group of notes. Remember that the first sentence of each paragraph should announce the topic clearly for the reader, as the *theory of relativity* model did on page 166.

Your notes should be organized in a logical sequence.

INTRODUCTORY AND CONCLUDING PARAGRAPHS

It is much easier to write an introductory paragraph *after* you know what the content of your report will be.

Your introduction should grab your audience's interest. It should also inform them about the famous person whom you will be describing.

As a class project, brainstorm different ways that you might use to introduce this report.

Do not end your report with the words *The End*. There are better ways to end a report. First, you might summarize the information you included in your report's body. Or you may state a personal comment on how you now feel about this famous individual after gathering all the information. The choice is yours.

As a class, you might brainstorm other ways to end your report.

STAGE THREE: REWRITING

Exchange your famous person report with a proofreading partner. Treat his paper as if it were your own. Be helpful. Use the **Checklist Sheet** as your guide.

You might also want to spot-check one paragraph using the **Sentence Opening Sheet**.

FAMOUS PERSON REPORT CHECKLIST

1. Is the report written in paragraphs? (Each paragraph must be indented.)

2. How did the introduction grab your interest? If it didn't, what could your partner include to make the introduction more interesting?

3. Since each paragraph should center on a different aspect of the famous person's life, give a name to each paragraph:

   Paragraph 1 _____
   Paragraph 2 _____
   Paragraph 3 _____
   Paragraph 4 _____
   Paragraph 5 _____
   Paragraph 6 _____

4. Are the notes grouped correctly? If not, identify the paragraphs that include out-of-place information. _____

5. What type of concluding paragraph did the writer use? How was it effective?

6. Check to see that the writer avoids fragments and run-ons. If you spot any, list the sentence number(s): _____

7. Any spelling errors? In which sentences? _____

8. Any punctuation or capitalization errors? In which sentences?_____

9. How well do the sentences flow together in each paragraph? Which paragraph flows the best? Which one needs work?

10. Is the report interesting and informative? What did you learn about the famous person that you didn't know before?

STAGE FOUR: PUBLISHING

FINAL COPY

Read your partner's proofreading checklist carefully. Make any changes from your first draft that you feel will improve your famous person report. Write a final copy in ink using your best handwriting.

FINISHING TOUCHES: BIBLIOGRAPHY, ILLUSTRATION, AND COVER

Since you used two or more sources to find information for your famous person report, you need to list them in alphabetical order. Your list of sources is called a **bibliography**. If you wrote down the necessary information while you were taking notes, the bibliography is almost finished. If you forgot to, it's back to the library to get it. Refer to page 159 for models showing how your bibliographic information should be written.

An **illustration** will add color to your report while showing the famous person's appearance. Draw your famous person, trace a picture of him/her, photocopy a picture, or cut a picture out of a magazine, if you have the owner's permission.

Make a **cover** of colored construction paper. The cover should include the title of the report in the upper middle; your name, class, teacher, and date in a list in the lower right corner. You may add a simple illustration if it fits nicely, or you can add color and design to brighten it. Your report should be in a booklet form.

Oprah Winfrey
middle of page

Niki Wagner
Language Arts
Mrs. Lynne Casey
April 8, 1999
lower right corner
